Heal Together Without Hurting Each Other

By: Derrick Jaxn

Table of Contents

Introduction

I cringe every time I hear someone tell a woman, "You need to heal!"

Not because the statement is problematic, but rather because it's usually a lazy recommendation that isn't coupled with further explanation on exactly what it means to heal and how to get there.

It's like hearing someone tell a broke person, "You need to be rich!" Or telling someone who's depressed, "You need to be really happy!"

Yes, most women and men need healing. To accomplish that goal, we also need to understand what it looks like when we are not healed, what it looks like when we are in the process of healing, and how we can tell when we are completely healed. This gives us clarity so we can effectively set a plan in place on how create an environment that makes the end goal achievable.

I've spent the last ten years obsessively studying and developing content that teaches individuals how to avoid situations they'll need to heal from. I've found that some believe healing is just another way of "getting over it" and letting go of a disappointing experience, but even in relationships, that's not the truth. Studies show that some relationship experiences can be just as traumatizing as surviving a natural disaster or going to war, especially betrayal. According to Dr. Shirley Glass, trauma recovery specialist and author of the book *Not Just Friends*, infidelity is the second most difficult relationship trauma to heal from, surpassed only by domestic violence, and requires the same path to emotional healing for the victim to love again.

Anything that compromises your ability to fully experience or contribute to a loving relationship, even a loving a relationship with yourself, is something that you'll need to heal from. This could be a previous relationship where you were controlled, manipulated, overly-criticized, abused, and more.

In my professional experience and through reading countless messages from my more than one billion online viewers, I've found that infidelity and infidelity-related betrayals are the most common experiences that leave a person with the task of healing.

Infidelity-related betrayals include loving a partner who watches pornography, gawks at other women or men online, carries on inappropriate conversation with the opposite sex, continues "friendships" with former flames, has wandering eyes, flirts with those of the opposite sex, or allows those of the opposite sex to disrespect the relationship in any way.

Yes, any of these things can require healing, and if you've been in a relationship with someone who has done these things, **you may need healing if**:

- You involuntarily reject the loving affection of your partner despite a conscious effort to receive it.
- Your vulnerability with your partner is coupled with a fear of being hurt, again, that you can't seem to shake.

- Someone can give you exactly what you ask for, but it doesn't result in the satisfaction you previously experienced.
- Despite wanting to be loved, being alone feels more comfortable than opening up to someone new or the person currently in your life.
- Disappointments in your relationship always evoke the thought of, "I knew it."
- Your guard is up higher with those who physically resemble those who've hurt you in the past.
- All it takes is one minor disappointment in a relationship for you to see that person completely different from that point forward.
- The thought of letting your partner in on your deepest, darkest thoughts and feelings terrifies you.
- Sex is not pleasurable despite your physical attraction to your partner, and there's no changes they can make to make it enjoyable.
- Negative expectations are in place until your partner disproves them, and even when your partner disproves them, the negative expectations come back soon after.

You'll know you're in the process of healing when:

- Your partner makes an effort to love you, and the feeling of fear or apathy is replaced with increased affinity for him or her.
- You notice an instance of vulnerability in a way you previously would've gone into your shell.
- The things you ask for are aligning with your deepest desires, and getting them are resulting in the satisfaction you were looking for.

- Your desire to be loved is resulting in neither a dependency nor an aversion to being alone, but rather an optimism around drawing closer to the ones who currently love you or openness to a new chapter with someone else when the time comes.
- Disappointments in your relationship are evaluated solely on the merit of the individual situation without being attached to how you measure yourself.
- You can notice a similarity between someone that once hurt you and a person you're looking at, but there is no emotion attached to the recognition.
- A minor disappointment is met with a premeditated plan for resolving the conflict, and once it's resolved, it no longer affects how you look at your partner.
- The thought of bringing your partner in on your deepest, darkest feelings comforts you in knowing he or she will love you regardless.
- Your sexual pleasure is correlative to your expressed needs being met, and past experiences don't mentally impose themselves on the moment.
- Negative expectations are replaced with critical consideration for someone new, and benefit of the doubt for the person you're in a relationship with, before their actions show you anything.

You know you are completely healed when these things become second nature instead of something you are making a conscious effort to create as your new normal. Otherwise, you are still healing just like the other 99% of us who have had to at some point.

While we're at it, let's go ahead and debunk a few more myths that have blocked blessings for those who have been hurt.

1. Being less than 100% healed doesn't make you less worthy of love. It just means that properly loving you won't be so cookie cutter, which isn't a requirement for someone who truly loves you anyway.

2. Just because you are healing doesn't mean you're broken. 'Broken' describes a person who refuses to allow healing in the areas they've been hurt and therefore will hurt everyone who tries to love them. 'Healing' describes a person who knows they've been hurt, but is doing the work to heal while protecting those who love them from that hurt with effective boundaries and open communication.

3. Time does not heal all. If you fracture a bone and simply let time pass, the pain will eventually subside, but true healing requires a reset first, therapy second, and protective measures going forward. The same thing goes for healing. Just letting time pass is not a healing method, it's a coping method. Coping is a part of the process, but far from the completion of it.

4. Pain-free does not mean emotional injury-free. Additionally, all pain-relief is not created equal. If getting rid of the pain comes at the cost of your long-term goals in life, relationships with those who love you most, or relationship with God, you're not healing, you're self-destructing.

5. Higher standards and more definitive boundaries as a result of what you've been through in the past doesn't mean you're "bitter." Your discernment of whom you trust is supposed to improve as time goes on. Your requirements for what it takes to earn your love are supposed to increase as you increasingly recognize the value of your love as well as the consequences of

giving that love to the wrong person. Yes, there are extremes to avoid, but putting additional measures in place to stop repeating the same mistakes over and over again is far from "bitterness." It's survival.

However, I'm not a believer in mere survival. I want all that God has for me, and I want the same for you--nothing less. I'm just tired of seeing the misguidance given to those truly striving to repair emotional damage they didn't cause. It has created a generation of people struggling to believe in love, or that they will ever find it.

Let's make something clear. True love exists; if you prepare for it and are open to it, it will find you. Also, if you've already found love, you don't have to put it on pause to rehab from wounds you've suffered. Flaws, scars, and all, you're enough right now for the love you deserve.

Chapter 1

Healing Isn't a Journey, It's a Fight

"Why don't marriages these days last as long as they used to?"

My reply: Women's standards are higher. Men's expectations haven't changed. Women's tolerance for nonsense is lower. Men's role models are fewer. Women aren't healing before being proposed to and are then realizing it during the marriage. Men are giving women too much to heal from and think proposing will erase the wounds. Most importantly, God is no longer at the center; our emotions are, both in the way we handle ourselves before marriage all the way until the time we decide to end it.

The original question was something I saw posted on social media, and while my reply got quite a bit of attention, it was another woman's answer to the original question that stuck out to me the most.

"Because marriage is overrated," it read.

After sifting through hundreds of other opinions on her sub-thread, her additional comments revealed that she once believed in marriage enough to jump the broom. However, something happened afterwards that turned her big day into a bigger regret, and from there, she adopted the popular, growing misconception that marriage is overrated.

A part of me wanted to respond, "Marriage isn't overrated. Intramarital healing is just underrated," but I refrained, partly because I didn't want to come off as insensitive, but mostly because people would likely have no clue of what I was referring to.

It's something I haven't spoken on, as I've always preferred to stick to what I know best--helping people avoid toxicity by recognizing red flags in the beginning and raising standards beyond what society says is acceptable. That works well for dating with a purpose and even sustaining a great relationship, but for many, the goal is Happily Ever After, which is a whole new ball game, and I've discovered that intramarital healing is the difference between those marriages that are real-life goals and those that turn into matrimonial scarecrows.

Again, this was something I didn't know or speak on much, but transitioning into married life forced me to take a deeper dive, and what I found was nothing short of treasure as well as a direct contradiction to the misconception of Self-Love.

Self-Love is supposed to be a fundamental approach to daily thoughts and actions that promote health, boundaries, and growth. Yes, that's necessary for a healthy life regardless of your relationship status, as I stressed in this book's predecessor, *Don't Forget Your Crown: Self-Love Has Everything to Do With It.*

However, the truth of Self-Love has gotten lost somewhere in translation and now flaunts a veil of bubble baths, detachment at the first sign of discomfort, and pridefully "fixing" ourselves in solitude in the effort to be strong.

While that misconception feels good for a moment and bubble baths are always nice, living a detached life doesn't equate to loving one's self, and emotional rehab can effectively happen with the help of the one you love.

"But you're supposed to heal before you get into a relationship."
"You shouldn't depend on anyone else to fix you."

If you're thinking anything close to the above statements, I totally understand where you're coming from, and so we're clear, I'm not promoting the idea that you should date while you are knowingly broken or go looking for others to fill any kind of void.

In a perfect world, your healing is complete before you meet the one you'll fall in love with. In a perfect world, once the healing is complete, there will never be another need for healing so long as the one you're with truly loves you. In a perfect world, the need for healing always has an end date, which surely comes before your wedding day.

Unfortunately, we don't live in a perfect world, but thankfully, there is a way for those who don't have a sparkly clean bill of emotional health to enjoy a healthy marriage or strong relationship that will lead to a healthy marriage.

If you're thinking, *"Well, I know that's not me. I'm completely healed from my past relationships,"* I humbly offer that if you've ever been through anything, especially a relationship betrayal, there's a chance some wounds from that experience are so deep, they won't be revealed until you're with someone who loves you deeply enough for both of you to discover them at the same time.

Or you may already be with that person and a wrong decision or series of decisions has led to a devastation you could have never imagined. A slow death like emotional neglect, or a sudden shotgun wound to the stomach like infidelity. You look at your spouse differently. You may even look at yourself differently, but you haven't given up, yet. You have no interest in remaining attached to someone who's no good for you for the sake of saying you're married, but if a completely new and upgraded relationship can evolve from this mess without divorcing, you want in.

Either way, the answer is the same: **heal together, without hurting each other**.

That's what intramarital healing is about. It's the opposite of both divorce and remaining in a toxic relationship; a joint effort that turns unimaginable pain into restored trust, reestablished safety, and intimacy like never before, especially for married couples or those preparing for marriage.

This isn't another book emphasizing how important it is to just forgive and forget. This is a book for those who truly want to forgive, would love to forget, but utterly refuse to repeat. This book is even for those who have nothing to forgive and forget in their current relationship, but have a previous season of their life causing thunderstorms in this one. This book will also help those who want to put parameters in place to prevent the most common events responsible for a need to heal.

Whichever situation you're in, you don't have to do it alone, and you shouldn't.

One of the most understated facts of Self-Love is that it's perfectly normal to need help in our healing and equally wise to get that help from those who are qualified to provide it. From both personal and professional experience, I highly recommend three sources of that help: God, a trusted relationship coach or counselor, and your spouse.

Some believe in relying solely on at least one of these, which, from the evidence I've seen, won't yield positive results.

Whether you're the one who's in need of healing, the ally to your spouse who's healing, or both, there's a strong likelihood that emotions are high, which means distortion of reality is real. So the two of you, alone, will do more damage by solely looking to each other for healing. This isn't rocket science, as most would wisely advise to consider a counselor or third party of some sort to help, but even that isn't enough.

World-renowned psychologist and best-selling author of the book *His Needs, Her Needs*, William Harley, stated that less than 25% of couples who received marital counseling felt like the counseling did them any good, and in many cases, made them more likely to divorce. I was in that "25% or less" category after sitting in sessions with incredibly competent professionals who could only account for what was told to them. They couldn't bring to our memory that which was lost in our earliest years, account for generational curses that predated any family members still alive, and their curriculums don't show how much marriage is as much of a spiritual contract as it is a legal one.

While I'm not one to force my beliefs on anyone, I'm also not one to shy away from the truth, and the truth is that including God in the healing process can make the seemingly impossible, possible. Notwithstanding, I utterly detest the notion of just "pray it away" when it comes to healing, be it in a relationship or in our individual mental health. God does, too, as the Bible repeatedly states how faith without works is dead and that prayer does not take the place of obedience, a.k.a., our actions to follow his instructions.

He gives many that provide a practical pathway towards healing, so any religious dismissal of mental and emotional damage in a marriage is just as problematic as believing we can circumvent the guidance of the one who created marriage.

"But just giving it to God IS enough."

For those who thought something like this, again, I understand your intention to acknowledge the limitless power of God, but no. It's not that God isn't capable of snapping his fingers and making everything shiny and new, but rather that God requires us to do more than simply give it to Him. Proverbs 11:14 tells us that we find safety in the multitude of counsellors, and James 5:16 states that we find healing in the confessions of our faults to one another. Truly giving your broken heart to God is to listen to His word that instructs us to involve the right people and in the right way.

This intersection between Godly guidance, vetted third-party help, and the teamwork of a couple who's in need of healing is at the core of everything we'll discuss. I didn't invent this process. I just discovered it, and the results I've personally experienced and professionally witnessed have been astounding. However, let's get something understood.

When it comes to love, it is not the thought that counts. It's the work that counts.

In fact, these principles have been utterly useless when one or both people refuse to do the work. The same thing is true for those who remain willfully ignorant to what it takes to effectively do the work, which primarily tends to be the man.

To some, that will sound biased, but look around at the world today and you'll see that when it comes to relationships, men are widely crippled by our ego and pride. If the topic is money or physical fitness or sports or something that fits the cultural identity of "manly", we're all ears on what we need to do to become world-class. But when it comes to meeting the emotional needs of a woman, especially one who is hurting, we act as if it's not our responsibility to continue evolving into better and more competent contributors than our previous generations. So, when we're knee-deep in these situations that we've never prepared for, we're lost on what to do and resort to temporary escapes, blaming our woman for not being emotionally bullet-proof, or walking away altogether.

Contrarily, women exhibit the exact opposite in terms of willingness to help a man heal, many times to their detriment.

In fact, a lot of women are currently healing from their attempt to try and help a man heal.

Shortly before writing this book, there was a famous pastor promoting the idea of a woman helping to raise her husband, and even worse, normalizing the suffering that resulted from it. In his words, "My wife went through more pain birthing me as a real man than she did birthing our two children." Even now, I want to throw up at the thought that there were millions who heard this and felt this should be the standard; men, walking into a woman's life and asking her for open heart surgery, then turning that scalpel that she just used to help him into a knife to cut her and leaving her to stitch herself up from the wounds he caused.

Of course, that's not every situation, but far too many to continue ignoring.

Instead of ignoring it, I'll primarily focus on equipping men to be the ally their wife's healing journey needs.

However, understand that your healing is not just a journey. It's a fight.

You're fighting for your peace. You're fighting for your ability to trust again. You're fighting to end the nightmares. You're fighting to eradicate the triggers, stop the flashbacks, and finally remove all fear of being hurt again. Even if it wasn't a fight you signed up for, it's a fight you're in, and you can win.

To ensure that you do, I've carefully outlined ways to safely bring your partner into your healing fight, while also giving you key indicators to know if he's simply not cut out for the job. That's the part no one wants to hear, but it's the reality we all must face. The good news is, if he's willing to put in the work, there's hope.

The misconception that "Marriage is overrated" didn't cultivate itself, and it won't erase itself. Nonetheless, for those who don't understand and act on the proper way to heal together without hurting each other, it will continue to be their truth.

My prayer and deepest desire for you as you read this book is that your truth will be far from that, but rather consist of the breaking of generational curses of toxic and short-lived relationships. My desire is that you walk away from this book relieved of whatever chronic emotional pain has lingered from your past, restored in your ability to love and be loved, and realigned with God's purpose for your relationship.

I've seen Bible scholars and psychology buffs alike coming up short when it comes to intramarital healing, but I've never seen someone who fully understood and bought into the actual work necessary come up short. With that, this book will heavily emphasize step-by-step measures to take for a new chapter in your relationship, but understand something; it is NOT a replacement for the word of God.

I encourage you to pray before continuing on that God speaks to you directly as you read so that His truth will be revealed specific to your situation on how you should apply the principles within these chapters. Verify, for yourself, that everything you read as well as the ways you plan to implement these principles align with God's word so this and anything you consume brings you closer to Him.

It's time for a shift. So, let's get started!

Chapter 2

Mistakes That Hinder Healing

"First off, stop making everything about you."

I'd had enough. After listening to a gentleman backstage of my seminar go on a ten-plus-minute spiel about all the horrors of trying to reason with his wife, I had to interject. It wasn't to be rude because I could see the sincerity on his face that he desperately wanted to absolve his marital dilemma that was created when his wife found out he'd had a little too much fun at his bachelor party, not outright cheating, but definitely blurred one or two lines before seeing her the next day to exchange "I do's." So, I figured my frustration with his naivety paled in comparison to his wife's, and continuing to let him talk about his distress was only enabling the damage he was causing at home with his hyper focus on how he felt about her healing process.

I didn't get the sense that he meant harm. He just genuinely had no idea, as many allies don't, on exactly what the situation was and how to avoid making it worse.

So, let's clear this up now before we go any further.

When a woman is fresh off of discovery of a wrongdoing, triggered from a previous wrongdoing, or both, the first thing you should do mentally is remind yourself of where you both are. In a general sense, the relationship that was feeling like a nice, warm, cozy home for her just turned into a battlefield, and this discovery is a stepped-on landmine. She's hurting, looking for cover, and clinging to anything that feels like safety along the way, even if it's not.

This is why I stress to women the value of dating men who are chivalrous, especially if she believes in being submissive to her husband once she's married. We stress submissiveness as a needed character trait for women, but men need to complement that. Contrary to popular belief, leadership isn't the complement. Although it warrants submissiveness, chivalry is the best evidence of character traits that balance out submissiveness. Why? Because more than just traditional gender-specific expectations, both chivalry and submissiveness indicate humility and selflessness. These two qualities take conflicts and turn them into understandings that bring closeness while selfishness takes those same conflicts and morphs them into toxicity.

So, back to the analogy. As an ally, you are on that battlefield as well as your wife, and your next series of moves will either establish you as her comrade, or her enemy. By default, you are her enemy, especially if you're directly at fault for the wrongdoing. But that position isn't permanent unless you force it to be by making one of the following mistakes:

1. Hyper focusing on self.

One of the most difficult tasks of an ally is focusing on the healing of your spouse while putting aside your own need for healing, especially in the height of her triggered state.

As an ally, you may need healing from some of the ways your spouse has mishandled her healing. At this time, it's tempting to get defensive, insert your feelings in so they're not ignored, or utilize other means of making sure you're acknowledged. But don't, at least, not right then.

We'll discuss more in-depth later about how and when to introduce your feelings, because they do matter, but we can only truly support the healing spouse with focus. Impulsively voicing your perspective will communicate a lack of regard for her feelings, a lack of protection for her best interests, and a lack of safety for her to restore the vulnerability she once enjoyed with you. Although you may be well intended, hoping to be transparent with what you're experiencing, sacrificing the opportunity to get your feelings off your chest in lieu of simply sitting with hers will prove your desire to emotionally show up for her more than your words ever could.

Again, your feelings do matter. Your healing matters. Your well-being matters. However, your spouse's healing is currently the focus, and if we don't focus, neither of you will experience the healing to your relationship that you seek.

Observe the feelings you're experiencing without engaging with them, and stay committed to the mission of seeing her healing through, trusting the process, and understanding that you will have the opportunity to safely integrate your healing into the relationship when the time is right.

2. Taking zero/partial accountability.

People make this mistake for different reasons, some because it's just impossible to believe they could be at fault for anything, while others make it because they genuinely don't see where they're at fault. No matter the case, it gets made often, and its negative impact on trust and healing is consistently damaging, so let's look at some examples of each so we can set them apart.

Zero/partial accountability: "I was wrong but…" (fill in the blank)
Accountability: "I was wrong. Period. What do you need to see from me to know that I mean that?"

Zero/partial accountability: "The only reason I even did that is because…" (fill in the blank)
Accountability: "No matter what, I shouldn't have done that."

Zero/partial accountability: "You left me no other choice."
Accountability: "Even if I didn't know a better alternative given the circumstances, I should have done more to prevent it from getting to that point or told you if it was getting there so you could decide on what you wanted to do."

Zero/partial accountability: "Okay, I can admit I was wrong, but you're not perfect, either!"
Accountability: "Yes, I was hurt by things you did, but absolutely nothing justifies what I did, and I apologize."

Zero/partial accountability: "The relationship already had issues anyway. This was just one of them."
Accountability: "Our imperfections didn't warrant my bad choices, and they don't justify them. We can address the other issues later, but right now, I want you to know that this wasn't your fault and you didn't deserve how I made you feel."

While it can be frustrating to feel like your spouse is overreacting to something you've done, or inadvertently putting themselves on a pedestal with the way they're expressing their hurt over your actions, refrain from trying to correct that in real time. However, do not just play the part. Actually be the part and take this opportunity of your spouse telling you that you're wrong as an opportunity to digest and grow from it with future actions that prove it. The alternative is a spouse who's shutting you out as she attempts to kill her expectations of you ever meeting her emotional needs, which gives you much less of an opportunity to help restore the relationship back to full strength.

There is a way to handle situations where you truly believe you're being framed, which we will discuss in later chapters, but for now, err on the side of full accountability first and foremost. This establishes your wife's well-being as your priority in her eyes, which is critical to her safety.

Any sarcasm communicated in the process will be no different from slapping her in the face and spitting in it afterwards. Those are strong words, but sarcasm in the middle of a fake effort to accept fault is an even stronger insult to her intelligence. Moral of the story: Don't do it.

3. Baby-stepping into full transparency, a.k.a., dripping the truth.

I get it. You don't want to hurt her more than you already have. You figured it'd be too much for her to handle. You were going to tell her everything but you lost the nerve midway through answering her question of, "Is there anything you need to tell me?"

Whatever the reason, it's a horrible one, so don't use it to justify telling partial truths over time. Transparency during the healing process isn't something you dip a toe into to test the temperature. Either dive in head first or risk drowning her trust in you, for good.

Whether the emotional injury happened within the relationship or prior to, the necessity of telling your entire truth up front remains the same. Not only is it necessary, but there's a compounding benefit to the rebuild of trust that goes understated.

As time goes on, those brutally honest truths about any and everything you've done in the dark will begin to lose their sting and finally start to rewrite a new story that you have nothing to hide. How? Like a revolving door moving 100 miles per hour, thoughts in a healing spouse's mind are circulating daily, trying to establish a truth that gives peace. The more lies, the less peace, therefore, the more time it takes to get through the healing process. Conversely, the more truths that begin to connect the dots for other questions you didn't know she had, the more peace is restored. The more those truths are coming directly from you in an effort to make sure she has nothing to guess about or privately investigate, the more her subconscious can accredit you for that increase in peace, and the more you shift from heartbreaker to heart healer. Before long, you'll be occupying a space in her mind that is capable and has a proven track record of telling her the truth, which she needs to be the version of her that can love you the way you need to be loved.

Consistent and unfiltered transparency nullifies the horror of her imagination about what you may be hiding, which can be just as convincing as reality when you've taken her confidence in what to believe.

4. Trying to convince her that she shouldn't be so worked up.

"You're overreacting."
"You're taking it too far now."
"You're doing too much."
"You're tripping."
"Is all that really necessary?"

Just an fyi, if you've said any of the previous statements, or anything similar, I'm here to tell you that it did everything but put your spouse at ease about whatever she may have raised concerns on.

Even worse if you tried to back this up with "logic", a.k.a., an unsolicited lecture about how the intensity of her reaction is not in correct proportion to the thing she is reacting to.

This isn't to say that a healing woman can do no wrong, and that she can go to any length to express her emotions about a situation that she's upset about. This is to say, there's a right and a wrong way to respond to her, and policing her is always the wrong way.

Instead of making this mistake, remind yourself that you are no longer convincing her to calm down. You are now to condition her to associate your presence with justified comfort. The difference is that instead of telling her in your own inconsiderately brash way that she should take a chill pill, you dignify her discomfort with more effort, patience, and solid evidence that will effectively calm her down over time.

Remember, this is a marathon, not a sprint.

5. Trying to do this without help.

If you're an ally reading this book or the healing spouse who'll be using the information shared to navigate this fight more wisely, then you're already on the right path. However, it isn't the end-all-be-all. You and your spouse need a mutual space to be together where someone can objectively evaluate your progress, make recommendations, and hold the two of you accountable.

Yes, you know your spouse better than anyone and it's not easy being vulnerable, but if you intentionally leave the fate of this healing process up to your perception while simultaneously being at the eye of the tornado, you're foolish, at best. The greatest athletes in the world rely on a coach to see things from a top-level view and manage the pace of the game.

Maybe finances don't allow for a coach right now. If so, see if you can find a mutual contact that you trust enough to be objective, yet is not too close to you nor your spouse to the point bias becomes a problem. If there's simply no one whatsoever within reach, then manage for now with the help of a potentially biased person that at least verbally commits to being unbiased, and keep the intel that they're given limited. The more his/her potential bias, the more boundaries for said person.

For instance, instead of telling this person, "My wife found my hard pornographic collection dating back to five years ago despite me telling her I hadn't watched porn since the day we got engaged. How would you advise us to go about rebuilding intimacy she feels like is no longer there?" You could say, "My wife is having a hard time regaining trust after a previous incident where she saw things in my phone that made her uncomfortable. What are steps you recommend in rebuilding trust so we can also experience intimacy again?"

If this third party is offended by your boundaries, they'd only do more harm than good with their "help," and you're better off managing while you can without them. If that's the case, then the last resort is to utilize the limitless resources of the Internet.

As you encounter hurdles or notice one of you are experiencing triggers, research trustworthy perspectives online that can help do damage control from either spouse stubbornly refusing to consider the other's perspective.

This doesn't replace the value of a third-party counselor or mentor, but it will assist in minimizing the implosions that high emotions on both sides tend to create.

6. Using good information in the wrong way.

This, like most of the mistakes on this list, tends to be committed by both the healing and ally spouse. Yet, again, we want to focus on allies right now, who sometimes make this misstep and therefore sabotage the entire process, either reverting back to square one or square *none* with a forfeiture by the healing spouse. Let's reference back to understanding where we're at, relative to the battlefield analogy. When you take good information and use it the wrong way, you go from just being an enemy, to an enemy whose strategy is to dress in camouflage, go into her bunker, steal her first-aid kit, and choke her with it while she's sleeping.

Simply put, you're weaponizing the resources being given to help her recover, thus risking the possibility of her refusing treatment from anyone no matter what it costs the both of you. Good counsel is hard to find, but good counsel that also has the trust of your healing spouse can be even harder to find. If you're using the assessments of your third party, this book, or even the Bible in a way that invalidates her needs, your spouse will cling to the perceived safety of getting away from both you and that information you've turned on her. Some call this rebellion. I consider this survival, or rather, the pursuit of it.

With that being said, there are times when your spouse will feel attacked despite you utilizing the guidance you've been given in its proper context. In these situations in which you notice you're now having to take cover in response to your attempt to use the trusted guidance, I recommend one of the following safety valves that will allow for a reset and revisit of the issue in a more productive space:

"Okay, maybe I misunderstood what was meant by that. Are you okay with us bringing this to our next session so I can gain clarity on the best way to go about this that protects both of our best interests?"

"Honestly, I'm not seeing this the same way you are, but that doesn't mean your feelings are invalid or that you're wrong. I simply feel differently right this moment, but I want to understand more about your feelings. Can we take some time so I can get more clarity from my trusted person?"

"Thank you for sharing your perspective. I'm not sure I see it that way, but I appreciate you sharing, nonetheless. Are you okay with asking for a second opinion on this from our counselor or one of our mentors?"

Of course, you don't have to follow this exact script, but essentially, you want to avoid the mistake of asserting that the end result of her feeling attacked was your intention, nor is it something you're comfortable risking doing again by solely relying on your own approach to rationalizing.

7. Mistaking light at the end of the tunnel for the finish line.

The urgency on getting through this difficult season of the relationship is going to be at what seems like an emergency-level high the entire time. Yet, you'll notice that as you and your spouse put in the work, there will be lapses of toxicity and distance that will feel like heaven on earth.

While there's nothing wrong with enjoying these moments and doing what you can to extend them when possible, don't

27

make the mistake of thinking the work is done. Couples who fall into this trap tend to get discouraged when they realize there's still a long way to go and become reluctant to allow more closeness in the future for fear of getting "blindsided" by reality, again.

As an ally, it's critical that you don't do this just as much as the healing spouse. One thing you can both remind each other regularly is, "This is going to take time. It's going to be up and down, rocky and smooth, etc. But I'm here for all of it, and I'm still just as committed to getting through this with you as I have been."

Note to the healing spouse: If you've noticed that your partner has done one or more of the things mentioned above, you may feel tempted to shove it in his face. However, don't. Not just because it's "wrong" but because it's ineffective and hurting you worse in the long run. I'll explain more later. You may honestly feel tempted to just leave, which may be warranted as well. However, for now, let's give the benefit of the doubt that just like you're a human experiencing this emotional roller coaster and trying your best to hold on, your husband is also on a roller coaster and doing his best to pull the lever to bring things back to a steady pace. Yes, we will primarily focus on bringing men up to speed as allies of their wives' healing, but they're powerless in this process without the help of their wives' help that will occasionally come in the form of grace.

Action plan:
Bring these points to your husband, and compassionately give him an opportunity to receive the information; how it's made you feel when he's done these things; and some small,

tangible improvements that would be meaningful to you over the next 30 days. Take note of any signs of defensiveness, ego, or reluctance. This is a chance for you to gather data of exactly what you're dealing with and whether it's safe to continue giving this process a chance or if it's wiser to create distance while you handle this yourself.

Again, this is all about safely bringing your partner into your healing fight, and without coddling or enabling. Safety is the end goal and current priority, and it's going to take two of you to establish that.

Chapter 3

The Empathy She Needs

"So ought men to love their wives as their own bodies. He that loves his wife, loves himself." Ephesians 5:28 KJV excerpt

One thing marriage has personally taught me is that when God emphasized empathy as a marital duty, it was for a reason.

Ephesians 5:28 describes empathy in the context of a husband loving a wife as his own body, or in other words, caring for a wife in the way that a husband would care for himself. To do that, he'd need to consider her feelings as important as his own, which requires empathy, something we can all see missing from both Christian and non-Christian marriages alike. I'd like to believe that's because the Bible doesn't go incredibly in-depth on its own, but again, God expects us to work with Him in producing fruit in our lives, and He's given us psychology to help when it comes to this concept.

Psychology recognizes three types of empathy: cognitive, compassionate, and emotional. Cognitive empathy is simply being able to understand someone else's perspective. Emotional empathy is sharing in the same feelings of someone else. Compassionate empathy is a mix of the other two, except turning that understanding and feeling into action that will help, which I've found is what most people need to effectively heal within their relationship.

Simply put, empathy in practice would be the act of one person viewing their partner's feelings in a validating, non-judgmental way that allows them to better protect their partner's feelings.

In theory this sounds good, but in real life when a wife is telling her husband she's upset, or hysterically showing she's upset, men often fall victim to the tunnel vision on how we feel about her being upset. This creates the part of the Rubik's Cube that confuses an appropriate empathetic response with one that forces the man to "be soft," or "give her a pass."

No.

Empathizing with your wife is one of the most critical steps in creating a healing environment for her as well as unlocking the version of her that will blow your mind with the love she gives you.

Let's look at the logistics. When a man empathizes with his wife, he's letting her know that her feelings are not only just as important his own, but they are also recognized for exactly what they are. This takes away any desire for her to defend how she feels because you've established that you care, and it also relieves her of the task of explaining to you how she feels since you proved that you know. Her defense and need to explain puts her in the same position as if she was dealing with a stranger who may hurt her and doesn't know her.

Well, what else can we conclude about a woman's demeanor when she's near a stranger? Reasonably, she'll keep one eye open around him, keep him from getting too close, refrain from being vulnerable, and hold back on giving her best to him.

This happens subconsciously in the mind of a woman during a relationship where there's no empathy, but the good news is, the exact opposite happens when the empathy is consistently present.

Instead of her subconscious registering that she's in the presence of a stranger, it will identify comfort, familiarity, protection, value, and even sacredness that's associated with being around a trusted loved one.

What won't a woman do for someone who is sacred to her and that she feels comfortable around?

For the women reading this book, I'd love for you to take this moment to validate the following answer I believe most women will give to that question: Nothing.

When a woman holds someone sacred to her and she feels valued by that person as well, not only will she do almost anything for that person, but the person won't even have to ask in most cases.

So, men, this means that whatever desire you have that doesn't dishonor her is virtually yours without question, but not without empathy.

This doesn't mean that you should be a doormat any time she's emotional or that you should pander to whatever her perceived feelings are. Empathy can be deployed even in disagreement, and when it is, it affords the opportunity for your disagreement to be respected instead of being dismissed.

Unfortunately, many men have a hard time qualifying their disagreement with empathy because they believe it should be enough to present "facts" about why they're justified in their disagreement.

"Would you rather be right or happy?"

I was on a panel of speakers several years ago when I heard one of the panelists present this to a gentleman in attendance. The guy in the crowd, who was about twenty-five years old, looked as confused as I felt when he replied, "I wanna be both!"

I was still only dating my now-wife, and hadn't grown to understand what the panelist who'd been married thirty plus years was saying, and he didn't explain to the crowd either. The time was up for the three-hour event, but I could tell by the panelist's head shaking that the guy in the crowd was still missing the point.

Shortly after getting married myself, I realized what was meant by the other panelist's question. He was challenging the young man to consider if being "right" was really his ultimate goal in dealing with his fiancée, or if there was something deeper that he wanted.

Those who struggle with empathizing for sake of being right in moments of high emotion tend to struggle because they don't understand what their deeper goal is, so they strive to achieve the one that pops up when things hit the fan, which is being right.

Here's an analogy that can better explain this. You have two keys in your hand. One of them is a silver key with the word "right" written on it. The other is a gold key with "empathy" written on it.

The silver key of "right" will unlock a mansion for two hours. The gold key of "empathy" will unlock a small box, and using either key will destroy the other.

Most men quickly go for the silver key that opens the mansion for two hours, except they have to leave two hours later, and they're back where they began. However, if men chose to use the golden key to open the small box, they would find in it the deed to the house that gives them multiple keys and the rights to the home to stay as long as they please.

Empathy doesn't always allow for you to prove that you're right in the moment, but it makes way for both you and your wife to come to understand what's right in the future, together, no matter who was right in that moment.

Empathy doesn't put you back where you began like trying to be "right" does, but rather elevates you and your wife's portfolio of assets, a.k.a., lessons learned that in turn yield dividends over the long-term.

The young man in the crowd was only trying to be "right", thus looking to walk in a mansion (feeling of bliss) that would soon come to an end when he realized his fiancée felt no closer to him due to him positioning himself as an emotional stranger to her.

If he was willing to destroy his silver key for that moment, he may have validated later that he was right in the beginning while bringing his wife to understand that not only was he right, but that he also had her best interests at heart in the process.

At worst, he would have been humbled in realizing he was wrong all along, but still would've ended *right* from the way he handled it.

You want love? You want respect, encouragement, trustworthiness, support, safety, best friendship, and life spoken into you? You want a wife who desires you constantly and who'll give herself to you freely in sexual intimacy with no question? You want a wife who never lets you doubt her loyalty no matter what?

All of these things are a byproduct of being connected, not being right, and empathy is the emotional pathway toward that connection.

"Okay, so how exactly do I empathize then?"

If you're asking yourself this question, follow the below steps for one pathway towards practicing compassionate empathy:

1. Any time you sense high emotion whether in your wife's words or behavior, ask God to posture your heart to be her emotional protector, not her prosecuting attorney.
2. Remind yourself that you could be completely clueless about what she's feeling or what she's

thinking. Otherwise, your assumption could show in your own tone as you speak, which will only make things worse.

3. If you're already in the middle of a disagreement, reassert to your wife that you're aware you very well may be wrong but you truly want to get this right because that is your goal, not being right. Getting things right between you and her is the goal. Make sure you mention that.

4. If you're not already in the disagreement, ask your wife if she's willing to talk, then proceed to let her know your current perception that something isn't right.

5. Once you have a confirmation from her, ask her to confirm if you have the right understanding of not only what she's expressing, but the feelings behind what she's expressing to you. This will establish cognitive empathy, which is good, but as we discussed earlier, not enough.

6. Take about three to five seconds to digest what she said. Literally pause for that time. This will slow the pace of the conversation as well as truly give you a chance to let her words sink in.

7. Articulate how you feel about the way that she feels, emphasizing the validity of her feelings and how you aren't satisfied in making her feel that way. Thank her for allowing you to better understand where she's at emotionally. If you still feel strongly about your original point, it's okay to say that, but this time, do so with reiteration that you don't intend to make her feel those negative feelings she's experienced, and make it clear that protecting her from those negative feelings is most important (if it is). If that's not your

truth, then simply make it clear that her feelings are still important and ask if she's willing to move the conversation to your next session with your third party.

8. Before ending the conversation, ask her, "How can I tangibly show you that I meant what I said in terms of how important your feelings are?"

From there, the execution is on you.

You may be wondering, *"Okay, but what about my feelings? They still matter, don't they?"*

The answer is yes, and temporarily managing them by putting them aside will allow you to protect them long-term as your spouse and your relationship with her heals.

A prime example of this is Ronnie and Tiffany. These two appeared in my inbox a little over a year ago at a standstill on a very simple disagreement--how many nights a week would be available for dates.

Ronnie worked hard and had finally gotten to a point in his career where things were starting to take off. With that, he felt like his wife Tiffany should be supportive in the form of sacrifice of time the two of them would ideally spend together. He felt like her expressing how much more time she wanted with him was her being unappreciative of all he was doing and all it would amount to in the future for both of them to enjoy both financially and in time they could later spend together.

Tiffany, on the other hand, felt like Ronnie shouldn't lose sight of his priorities just because success was now gaining momentum for him. In fact, the more time he spent chasing his success, the less significant she felt, and the more she fought for time with him, the more it hurt because this was something he once treated like a privilege. With time, it seemed to have regressed to a chore he felt like he'd just get to later when he was eventually doing what really mattered to him.

Both of them had a common grievance of feeling taken for granted but couldn't see past their emotions to find the solution, especially Ronnie. It's not that his feelings were less valid than Tiffany's, but they were blinding him from his own life goals he originally made. Meanwhile Tiffany's feelings were directly aligned with achieving those goals. Ronnie's focus had changed, not Tiffany's loyalty, but through his own emotion he couldn't see that the more he held on to his own selfish point of view, the more he was losing the woman who was the key catalyst to everything he was chasing.

Ronnie had quickly forgotten how Tiffany was a major reason success was even a real possibility with all she'd done to encourage, support, and invest into his dreams of being a successful entrepreneur. Without her, he would've lost his confidence many losses ago. Without her, he would've been short the money to make ends meet in those times his ideas didn't turn a profit. Without her, he would've burned out in times he couldn't afford to pay employees while at the same time not being able to do all the things his business needed by himself.

The sacrifice Ronnie required from Tiffany was the same sacrifice she'd already given him when no one else believed in him, and was still willing to give so long as he kept her needs a priority. That was the steam in her engine that provided the energy she needed to keep supporting his dreams. She needed to know that she played a valued role in his journey and also held a secure place in his future.

But the more Ronnie got caught up into his ambition, the more he snatched the rug Tiffany stood on from under her feet to keep his dreams moving closer to him. She no longer felt valued, as he didn't make time to show her she was. She no longer felt secure as the time that was previously reserved for her seemed up for grabs for anything that would pop up on his schedule. Not to mention, the more success she helped him acquire, the more attention he attracted from other women, thus requiring a higher level of discipline from Ronnie that he invested no energy into developing.

So, while Ronnie's feelings were real, the picture those feelings painted of the issue was not. Yet, because he made the mistake so many of us make, he was more married to his own perception than he was his spouse's well-being, which left Tiffany to eventually shift into survival mode.

Survival mode takes on different forms for everyone. Sometimes it means resorting to toxic coping mechanisms that feel like an escape, be it sex, drugs, alcohol, or some other experience that provides a distractingly intense gratification that creates regret and dependency in its wake. For others that survival mode looks like lashing out in the form of verbal or physical abuse, sabotaging the relationship, or for Tiffany, it looked like what I call 3D Behavior:

disgruntled, dissatisfied, and distant. This is where a woman has less love to give because it has been wasted, less emotional investment since it no longer feels valued, and less emotional presence because her emotional state is increasingly negative, which is an unbearable place for anyone to exist in.

Ronnie and I were able to get on a call so I could explain Tiffany's position in a way he needed to hear it, as a man. I could relate to him and knew that if it could just click, it'd turn everything around for him.

As an entrepreneur, I knew how difficult it was to make the time needed to both thrive in my career while giving my family the time they needed. Some people say there's no way to do both, but that's a lie. It all comes down to the priorities, and structure to make sure those priorities are kept. For me, this meant making a schedule that I shared with Ronnie as a baseline for what he could model after and tweak according to Tiffany's needs. This is a simplified version of that schedule, specifically on a day where I needed to work.

3:00am | Wake up
3:15am | Prayer
4:00am | Gym
6:00am | Back home/Breakfast
6:30am | Work
8:30am | Wake the children, brush their teeth, make them breakfast
9:00am | Back to work(while wife takes over for children)
12:00pm | Lunch date with wife while sitter takes children
1:00pm | Personal time with wife/nap
2:30pm | Work

6:00pm | Family time. No work whatsoever.
8:00pm | Help bathe kids, put them to sleep and tidy up the home
9:00pm | Shower and wind down with wife
10:00pm | Sleep

Again, this is just my schedule, and this was something that worked for my wife and me. This gave her the amount of time she needed with me while also allowing me the time needed to handle my business and get my rest. This also required me to cut down on or completely end many time wasters like social media and responding to every message that got sent from those who didn't have a lot going on in their lives.

For Ronnie, those time wasters were video games and YouTube videos about conspiracy theories. It's not that these things were necessarily bad (if that's what you're into), but Ronnie needed to put them in their place on the priority list if he was going to stop Tiffany from feeling like she was in last place, and he did.

In the past year since our conversation, he and Tiffany have reported that his compassionate empathy completely changed the environment of their marriage. Through self-reflection, she realized she was triggered by his shrugging off her needs for quality time since that was the issue in her previous relationship before finding out her ex was giving his time to other women. But Ronnie was not only faithful, but now willing to actually give her the time she needed, both reducing her triggers and communicating in her love language.

He realized that by giving his wife more of what she needed, it motivated her to go above and beyond to support his career. She didn't just let him work when it was time for him to, she found ways to help do admin work and prepare him for the next day. She got her friends and family to support his new products. She even hired and trained a virtual assistant to help him manage his increase in emails and other menial tasks.

Just by empathizing with his wife, Ronnie was able to turn his life partner to his power player for everything he was originally trying to accomplish. Tiffany was able to heal from the past relationship trauma of being chosen over by her ex because now she had a husband who put her first, second only to God. They're far from the finish mark, but just a simple adjustment from a genuine place of empathy made a world of difference.

However, most men struggle realizing this truth because along the way, they're distracted by how upset they are to have to shift so much around in their lives. Not only are they upset, but empathizing while being upset makes them feel emotionally obsolete. If this is you, don't be fooled by your frustration. Your feelings are not obsolete. You're just growing to a point where they don't control you, but rather you control them.

Remember, one of the signs that a healing spouse is making true progress is when he or she can begin to replace feelings of fear with feelings of increased affinity in response to the ally spouse's efforts to love.

Your control over your own emotions develops emotional intelligence. Emotional intelligence opens the door for true compassionate empathy. The empathy then kicks fear out of your spouse's heart and invites the healing to come in and make itself at home. That healing will come in and tell your healing spouse's love that it's safe to come out of hiding. That love will abound, allowing your feelings to be acknowledged and taken care of better than before.

It's all connected.

This isn't something people typically have or don't have, but something we have and then lose the more familiar we get.

Think about in the dating phase when you were careful about your words and how they made her feel. When you asked her if she was uncomfortable every five minutes the first time she came to your home or was alone with you. When you noticed a facial expression was less than pleased and you asked questions to get to the bottom of the issue before going further. If she was sick, you focused less on how you had plans of going out for the weekend and more on the type of soup and hot tea she needed to feel better.

These were all moments of compassionate empathy, at least pieces of the foundation that would allow for it. Your wife likely considered you "husband material" because of what you did to identify with how she felt, pushing your own feelings temporarily to the back, and then acting in a way that showed that her feelings mattered.

But, at some point, you got familiar, and with familiarity came complacency. At that same point, she began shielding how she felt from you because your focus on how you felt only made her feelings worse.

If you still have confusion around showing empathy, simplify it by removing the complacency. That will put you on the right path and keep you there so long as you stay consistent.

Note to the healing spouse: Based on the information above, did you find yourself feeling like there's no way your spouse could ever truly empathize with you? If he hasn't yet, then there's a good chance you don't see how, but here's one way to know for sure. Ask him if he'd be willing to discuss this chapter with you. If not, then ask him to let you know why. If his answers are laced with his own preferences of how to do things, what he believes should be addressed first, etc., then he's telling you how he feels about potential ways to better love you, he's not interested. However, if he's at least intrigued on the strength of hearing how this is something you'd like him to check into, you've got something to work with.

Action plan:

For seven days, set aside one hour a day to have a difficult conversation about something he's troubled about. This will allow him an opportunity to feel strong emotion and work to reign it in so he can focus on yours.

For example, he takes issue with something you said to a family member of his recently.

In that hour, he's to go through the steps listed earlier in the chapter. If it gets too heated, call it a day, and retry the same topic the next day. If things remain calm enough to complete the steps, grade him on his execution of showing true empathy on a scale of one to 10 with 10 being absolutely amazing. Tell him how it made you feel to now know he has the ability to empathize and ask him how he feels about doing this going forward. It's common to be a bit uncomfortable since it's new, but it gets easier as time goes on. This is the process of him being equipped with the empathy needed to help you facilitate your healing.

If he scores below a six for the entire week, continue the exercise two to three times a week going forward. Be clear with what he can do better, and if you don't see genuine effort, then accept that as a clear indicator that he's not concerned about your safety nor your healing.

Chapter 4

Loving Her While She (Seemingly) Hates You

There's a difference between moving on from a hurtful occurrence in your relationship and trying to skip over the hurtful occurrence in your relationship.

Attempting to skip over it is the effort to ignore any of the four steps to properly process it first, which are acknowledgement, apology, verbal commitment, and consistent action.

One thing many of us underestimate is how much consistent action it will take for the moving on to officially happen. For some, this time is only a few months, while for others, it's several years. While the healing spouse typically wants to move on just as much as the ally wants her or him to move on, sometimes it doesn't seem that way.

I had a sit-down with my mentor and his wife of thirty-nine years, and they told me about one of the most tumultuous seasons of their marriage. It all started when he was only seventeen years old. He had a child by a woman who told him she didn't want him in the child's life being that he didn't have a lot of money, and by the time the child was born, she had begun seeing a man who did have a lot of money and didn't want to make that man uncomfortable.

That's correct. She propositioned to kick a biological father out of his son's life in exchange for a man with money. Regrettably, my mentor, John, obliged and shortly thereafter met his current wife Sonya.

Early on, Sonya expressed to John that she would not want a man who had children being that she didn't want children either, so he never told her about his child. However, his entire family knew, and they helped him keep his secret.

Fast forward about fourteen years later and John ran into his child's mother that he hadn't seen since he was there at the birth of their child. As "luck" would have it, she and her then-boyfriend had married but later divorced, so she no longer saw a reason for John to continue missing out on his son's life. For sake of the benefit of the doubt, I would think his child's mother had also grown to see how erroneous her decision was in the same way John had seen how erroneous his was. Nonetheless, he had a new decision to make and that was to either deprive himself and his son of a relationship so that he wouldn't risk costing himself his marriage or start the relationship with his son and risk losing everything he had built with his wife Sonya.

John decided that the right thing to do would be to finally start the relationship with his son he never should have agreed to hinder from the beginning, even if it put him at risk for losing his wife Sonya.

Sonya described the moment she found out about her teenage stepson as one of the most crushing experiences of her life, even more so than the death of close loved ones over the years. Understandably, her trust was broken in John, as well as everyone in his family who knew about the child but never told her over the thirteen years they had been married.

She said it was more than five years before she found it in her heart to forgive John and build a relationship with the child who John had fathered as a teenager.

In those five years, Sonya admits she was completely cold, detached, and almost hateful toward John. Although she doesn't describe her actual feelings toward John as hatred, she couldn't deny the similarities between her day-to-day treatment of him and that of someone she hated.

John then affirmed that those years were some of the most difficult years of his life, not just because of her hurtful actions, but because he had no idea when they would end, or if they ever would.

The moral of the story is, as a husband, you don't get to set the timer for how long it's going to take your wife to recover from something you did to hurt her.

While it may be wrong for her to lash out at you day after day, especially after verbalizing her forgiveness and the commitment to move forward, verbal apologies are just the beginning of a healing process for the emotionally healing partner, something both of you would be wise to keep in mind.

The problem with "forgiveness"

There's a misconception about forgiveness that once it's expressed, it's done. From there, the obligation is on the betrayed person to act according to their expressed forgiveness while the betrayer simply holds up his or her promise to not commit the same crime.

That would be true if we only lived through a hurtful experience once, but we don't. Once we suffer at the hands of someone we love, we relive that experience every time we're reminded of it. Our brain re-creates the scenario, which reproduces the hurt and anger and before we know it, we're back in the same position we were in when we initially became aware of the betrayal. That's why we have to "snap out of it" when we get lost in thought about something in our past. Our brain teleports us back in time, leaving only our physical bodies in the present moment. Meanwhile, our hearts are subject to the same excruciating stimuli produced by the past experience. For anyone who's suffered a major relationship devastation, this can become a way of life, a.k.a., a living hell.

So, forgiveness as a one-time, click-of-our-heels magic trick is misleading because the experience doesn't just happen one time.

The betrayed partner needs to understand this, but as the ally to her healing, so do you. She has to forgive you every time she looks at you and wonders how you could be so careless with her heart. She has to forgive you when she's triggered by something you two once did that was meaningful, but not meaningful enough to keep you from hurting her. She has to forgive you every time she sees the friend or enemy that she defended you against who was right about you after all. She has to forgive herself for not seeing through your efforts to hide your wrongdoing.

She also has to forgive you for things you didn't even do, but possibly could've done. Why? Because you took her trust that kept these possibilities from haunting her.

The list goes on, unfortunately, but the point is, there are hundreds of instances of forgiveness she will be responsible for all from one infraction in order for you to experience what we characterize as forgiveness. The more convinced she was that you wouldn't put her in this position, the more that number of times she will have to forgive you increases, and therefore the more of a process real forgiveness becomes.

Another misconception of forgiveness is that it's the singular key to closure over a hurtful situation. As if once a betrayed partner forgives, his or her peace of mind will return back to normal. No. While forgiveness is one of the keys to closure, the other key that's rarely discussed is the ability to seal our expectations of being hurt again.

Sealing our expectations of being hurt means compartmentalizing them away in a particular time that we're no longer in or to a particular set of circumstances that are no longer present. In this, the expectations of being hurt are no longer triggering fear responses that need to protect us by keeping our minds running overtime.

From my experience, I've noticed three elements involved in sealing our expectations when it comes to relationships:

1. Knowing a person who hurt us is no longer in our life.

2. Knowing a person who hurt us, but remains in our life, is no longer the version of themselves who hurt us.

3. Knowing we have a better understanding of what hurt us, therefore giving us the power to prevent it from hurting us again.

A person who is seeking closure is pursuing the ability to anchor themselves in one of these elements. However, forgiveness, alone won't achieve this, so some people are left believing nothing can, which is untrue. We just need to understand the pathways to achieve closure and commit to the steps to get there.

Before we go any further, please understand that I'm not referencing "closure" in the traditional sense of waiting for someone else to come hand us a permission slip to move on. That's what most people treat closure as, and it keeps them powerless over their emotional and mental well-being. They wait, beg, cry, wonder, and hope that the one who hurt them will come rescue them from their spinning thoughts with answers to all of their questions and convincing apologies. While intramarital healing should provide that, it still won't give you closure.

Real closure, according to Webster's dictionary, is the comforting or satisfying sense of finality victims experience. Emphasis on "finality." **The key to closure is establishing the belief that a hurtful experience or season in your life is final.** That's all you need, and you can achieve this with or without the help of the one who hurt you.

For those who are healing from a previous relationship, the first and third elements are the only ones needed to achieve closure once the forgiveness process is complete. Kick them out of your life and learn from the experience. Once you've done both, you may still require additional healing, but you will have closure on that situation.

Ninety percent of dating advice teaches from this perspective, but when you're in a serious relationship or marriage, you don't wipe your hands with the one who hurt you. You join hands with them once they prove they're ready to hold the precious gift of your love within. You must also train yourself to see them as a different version of themselves from the one who hurt you.

Unlike the others, this isn't a one-man (or woman) job, but often, in a desperate desire to move on from a hurtful experience, the betrayed partner will take on 100% of the responsibility of this task.

If a woman has been cheated on but truly believes her partner is remorseful, she will do the work of both forgiving him and trying to force herself to see her man differently. She will even blame herself when she fails to see him in the light she once did. Subconsciously, she will struggle to open up to, be comfortable with, or even respect him the way she once did. This will confuse her since she knows she's done the work to forgive, yet not experiencing the fruit of closure from the past that allows her to fully step into the new season of their relationship.

This is where the ally comes in, understanding that forgiveness is not only a process, but only half the battle.

With that understanding, you also understand why you may not always receive the grace that you expect from a woman who genuinely forgives you for your wrongs.

In fact, you may experience many occasions where it feels like your healing spouse downright hates you. Her frustration, pain, anger, and pursuit of an emotional state where she feels in control, again can materialize as a wrath like no other.

Hell hath no fury like a woman scorned.

Now that we have a better understanding of what inspires a woman's wrath, let's deal with the reality of it. Sometimes, the only thing you can do is hold on for dear sanity.

As an ally, you can either resort to escapes in the form of vices that will only make things worse. Or you can search for strength to grow this incredibly difficult season.

We know what escapes are: alcohol, drugs, other women, etc. We also know that these indulgences will only add fuel to the already blazing fire.

So, let's discuss the ways an ally can draw strength from this instead, which I've witnessed come through God, Godly support from those who are vetted for the best interest of the relationship, and reminders as to why the wife is worth being strong for.

When you're ridden with guilt, discouraged about the future of the relationship, and ready to just start clean with someone who can wipe away your sins as quickly as God does, convincing yourself she or any woman is worth it can be difficult.

I can't make that decision for you, and no one else can, but I will offer you this much; if your wife's entire life was thrown off when she was made aware of what you did to hurt her, or up until this point she's sacrificed and trusted your leadership in ways that changed the course of her entire life, or if you know that if the world was to end in one hour, that she is the one you would want to spend that hour with, chances are you have a woman who is worth it.

Why? Because it's not that those types of women are rare, but a woman like that whom you are compatible with and attracted to who also allows you into such a space in her heart is rare.

The fact that having all of those in one woman is rare is not going to make it much easier for you to endure all that comes with the expression of her anger and her hurt, especially if it drags on for several months or even years. Yet, it should keep things in perspective as you protect your blessing over the long-term and help make right what you wronged.

Something the healing spouse will come to realize is that at some point, her anger and hard heart are no longer protecting her, but keeping her from the love that will protect her. She will understand that any vengeance or evening of the score can't soothe her the way the reopening of that door to your love will.

Now, if things have escalated to a point of physical abuse or danger for anyone in the household, it's not a matter of whether or not she's worth it. You may simply have to leave while God works on her heart until it's safe to come back together with the guidance of a trusted counselor or third party.

If the wrongdoing was some kind of betrayal, like for instance, infidelity, it's important as the ally, that you remember your admission of guilt was much more than a moment of transparency for you. It was the beginning of questions for her as it relates to her worthiness of being loved in the same way that she loves you, her worthiness of faithfulness, her attractiveness, what else you may still be hiding from her, when the next time will be that you will do this again, if she will ever wake up without the painful agony of this new reality of still being in love with somebody that hurt her more deeply than she could have ever imagined, her embarrassment from how much she believed in you, and triggers that she can't even begin to understand.

There are many variables in a situation like this, so don't underestimate the complexity of this process. For instance, if there are elements of a baby that is now in the equation, an STD, or if people she knows personally were involved, that could certainly extend the amount of time and increase the volatile nature of the process. Nonetheless, it's important that you, as a husband who is deeply remorseful, sincere in his intentions to learn from his mistakes, and never, ever, hurt his wife so deeply again, that you remember most marriages include infidelity at some point, and thousands recover from it every year.

Yours can, too, so long as you avoid two traps that many men fall victim to.

The first trap is what I call the Bootleg Handyman trap. A bootleg handyman in this context is one that ignores the context of the situation and the part they played in it by jumping to "fix" what is broken without having a clue on how badly it's broken.

You become a bootleg handyman when you skip empathy, ignore the new vantage point that you've given your wife of who you may be, and try to fast-track the restoration process. While well-intended as you may be in this situation, the harder you try to fix things with her by immediately shifting into good-guy mode, lecturing her on how not helpful it is that she continue to react to that hurtful situation, or even worse, attempt to restore normalcy by imitating it, a.k.a., acting like nothing happened, you may be furthering the divide between you two until there's enough room for a divorce attorney to squeeze in.

I had a friend who fell into this trap. We'll call him Fred for the sake of anonymity. While this was before marriage, the same concept applies. He and his fiancée Jessie whom he'd been with for three and a half years, were expecting a baby, and during the last two months before giving birth to their son, Fred cheated. While he allegedly felt awful about stepping out on his fiancée and didn't continue in his cheating any further than the day it happened, it was nothing in comparison to how he felt when one of the last checkups for his fiancée revealed that she had contracted Gonorrhea from Fred.

How Fred felt was nothing in comparison to how Jessie felt as she found out about this while carrying their son, still needing his support, trying not to get so upset that it could hurt the baby, all while questioning her future with Fred, among all the other tormenting thoughts of someone who experienced such a level of betrayal. Unfortunately, Fred jumped into bootleg handyman mode like Michael Phelps on his way to win another gold medal.

Over the next few months, he spent half of his 401k on the baby shower, a new Mercedes Sprinter van for their family, and even had the baby's room renovated on the level you would expect of a high-profile celeb's first child. He cooked dinner every night for his fiancée when he got home from work and cooked all three meals from scratch on his day off. He made sure that his fiancée could want for absolutely nothing both before and immediately after the birth of their son. However, all she wanted was to turn back the hands of time to the day before she met Fred so she could walk away.

Of course, that's harsh to say, but that's the reality of a woman who's been crushed by a man that she loves deeply, and then sees him being the man that she wanted all along but only in a temporary effort to gain a clear conscience about his deception. To make matters much worse, Fred would sometimes berate her for not jumping for joy over the things he did to earn back her favor. The insult to injury of his expressed disappointment and the fact that all those great gestures came to a complete halt when he got tired of waiting on his parade was the last straw.

After somehow managing to get through the rest of the pregnancy, give birth to their healthy baby boy, and surviving the initial months of having a newborn to look after, his fiancée was no further in recovering her unbroken heart than when she had first begun. The STD was gone but the pain was far from it, and after several months of being guilt-tripped for not bouncing back to her old self on Fred's schedule, she officially called the wedding off and later left Fred for good.

It's important to note that the problem isn't that Fred was on his best behavior. If you're in this situation, that's exactly what should be and do so with the intentions to make this your new normal. Of course, you'll be riding emotion in the beginning, but sustain the reinvestment of your energy you used to spend peeking outside your relationship to water your own grass, even if your wife spits on your lawn every chance she gets. .

The problem is the fact that Fred was only on his best behavior in an effort to ease the ramifications he felt from hurting Jessie and furthermore persecuted her for not responding as favorably as he would have liked. After persecuting her, he went so far as punishing her by completely going cold, and there's no telling what else he was doing in that time as well.

With that, she had zero reason to believe that he had the awareness and/or conviction to not repeat the same offense at some point in the future, in which she knew she could not handle ever again.

True to the bootleg handyman mindset, Fred utterly refused any proper training or guidance that could have otherwise saved his family despite Jessie's repeated recommendations. Instead of undergoing personal therapy, requesting joint therapy for the two of them guided by a mental health professional, marital books, or most importantly, turning his life over to God and away from the world permanently, Fred tried to take matters into his own hands.

Granted, the road towards recovery for Fred and Jessie would have been long even if they took the right steps from the very beginning. Yet, she was willing to try until Fred's immovable pride and childish tantrum towards the end killed all hope.

The second trap a lot of men fall into is even worse. Let's call it the Score Settler. This is where the oblivion of a heartbreaking situation is taken to a level that exceeds mere naivety and exposes even more of the unreadiness for a loving relationship of the offender.

In this trap, the offense is so quickly forgotten by the wrongdoer that soon after, he convinces himself he's the victim when his woman's hurtful reaction goes on longer than he expected. It usually goes something like this: A man deeply wounds his woman whether knowingly or unknowingly. They discuss it. She forgives him. They attempt to return back to life as normal, but occasionally lose that battle when triggers are activated or she simply has an off day. Since the original wrongdoer set a timer for how long that should be permissible, he expunged his record and convinces himself that her actions are strictly a byproduct of her character.

While she, the actual victim, wants to honor her expressed forgiveness, that unfortunately doesn't absolve her of being a human being who is still hurting. However, the actual offender has already given himself a completely new slate, which he thinks comes with a new unbroken heart for her, and now feels justified to in some way, settle the score. So, that means he gives himself a pass to re-injure her emotionally due to her reaction from his original injury, and honestly, he was going to do it again at some point in the future anyway.

Now both of these traps have something in common and that's the ignorance that primes their prey. One's ignorance translated into futile attempts to reconcile while the other's ignorance translated into malicious attempts to serve justice. Nonetheless, both are rooted in ignorance.

Unfortunately, very few people are teaching both our young boys and young girls about the ramifications of acting out of a moment of lust, pain, or unforgiveness. So, generation after generation is being groomed to believe that all is well once the words "I'm sorry" leave your lips for something you've done to hurt another person. However, one thoughtless moment or a season of thoughtless moments can create a lifetime of loss, regret, and health-altering aftermath.

So, to all the men out there who are on a seemingly endless road towards "back to normal," your frustration is understandable but far from warranted. If your wife has at least verbally committed to trying to make the marriage work with you and currently not putting your life or anybody's life in danger, you should see your everyday struggle, no matter how uncomfortable it may be, as an extension of grace from God.

Now, it's important that we talk about exactly what that discomfort could entail so that this book is not a continuation of ignorance for those who are unaware of what to expect.

There are some women out there who, no matter how badly they've been treated, could never do to someone else what's been done to them.

And then there are women who reach their limit and snap. At least, that's how it seems. What's really happening here is the "anger" stage of grief.

In 1969, Elisabeth Kubler-Ross introduced the five stages of grief to explain how people cope with illness and dying. The five stages were denial, anger, bargaining, depression, and acceptance. Since that time, studies have evolved revealing additional stages of shock and hope, but most importantly that the grieving process can happen any time a person experiences great loss, including the loss of their perception of a person.

These stages aren't linear, meaning they can happen in any order, and some people don't experience all of them. However, if you deeply hurt your wife and she begins doing things out of her normal character with seemingly no conscience about it, it's likely that she's now in the anger stage of her grieving.

In this season of her healing, you could spend months or even years giving her the best of your love and seeing her throw every ounce of it down the toilet. She may disparage your name to those you know and those you don't know. Those people will likely become a fueling source for more resentment towards you, and because the bond is broken, you'll only be left to wonder. She may find another man to befriend in this time, just to see if she likes the feeling enough to go with it, which could happen as well.

She may purposely jump at the opportunity to humiliate you and make you feel less than a man. If she feels your hopes getting up about finally making it through the storm, she may self-sabotage until you're frustrated, hurt, or even angry enough to throw in the towel, or even entertain thoughts of suicide.

Letting her know how bad it's gotten for you or even how suicidal you are won't help either. If she's cold enough, it'll only feel to her like long overdue justice and she won't lose an ounce of sleep knowing that you're on edge.

If you don't lose your mind, she may see it as a challenge and look for ways to sabotage you professionally or ruin the enjoyment you had in your hobbies. If her and her ill-chosen support group's mind can conceive it, then you'd better be ready for it. Those moments of seeing you in absolute agony will be the closest thing to relief she'll experience, and if she's hurt badly enough, she'll get as much as possible.

Let's be clear, none of these actions are justified.

In fact, they are destructive, toxic, and can even cross the line of mental abuse. They are not helping her heal and they are not supportive of your efforts to be an ally in her healing. However, they represent the reality of deeply hurting a woman who only had intentions of loving you.

Let me also make clear, that as much as she may enjoy the instant gratification of seeing you hurt to some degree as much as you hurt her, no woman is voluntarily remaining in a place where she craves the satisfaction of seeing you hurt. The only reason it even feels good in a moment is because the pain she's masking feels too unbearable to allow to surface.

So, then, what is the solution?

In addition to relying on God, Godly counsel, and reminders of why she's worth it, you cannot afford to lose yourself, unless you're losing yourself in Christ, which hopefully you try to do daily.

What I mean is, don't get caught up in this situation and lose what makes you who you really are when you are your best self. That doesn't mean don't cry, don't hurt, don't feel. That means don't stay so focused on the situation that you create a prison in your own mind that you can't escape from to live life in any other capacity besides dwelling on the circumstances that are in front of you.

Losing yourself leads to feeling like life isn't worth living, but that doesn't mean you need to end your life. That means you need to end the process of losing yourself. So, if you notice that you don't eat the same, can't go to work anymore or focus when you're at work, don't hang out with your friends, stopped doing things you used to enjoy, no longer care to look or smell nice, relate everything wrong in life to some negative aspect of yourself, can't sleep at night, or find yourself at the mercy of your wife's mood, then you've already begun the process of losing yourself.

This is a time to give both you and your wife a break.

Maybe forty-eight to seventy-two hours to simply decompress should get the job done, but if your mental state is in critical condition, take a week. Gently, let her know in advance that you'd like to do that without turning the conversation into the way she's made you feel. Chances are, she'll be so numb, she'll jump at the opportunity to tell you how she doesn't care, and it'll be genuine. Don't expect to see an ounce of regard for your emotional well-being whatsoever, unless it's her salivating for the chance to see you break right in front of her eyes.

I know that sounds cold-blooded, but her blood is cold at the moment and there's nothing you can do about it in the immediate future. However, don't focus on that; focus on absolute surrender to Christ and self-preservation.

Absolute surrender is difficult yet liberating in the darkest of seasons. It involves a process of almost obsessively seeking the face of God in the form of worship, prayer, and reading of the Word. I know this sounds "preachy," but it may save your life if you've nearly become a martyr for your wife's healing.

The fact that you have deeply hurt your wife and undoubtedly deserve reprimand for it does not make you deserving of a slow death penalty. While some may disagree, God's grace is for all. When He came down in the form of His son to die for you, it wasn't because he didn't care, and if God sees you as worth caring for, then who are you to not care for yourself?

Furthermore, our mistakes have a funny way of lying to us about who we are and our future. The guilt, shame, and seemingly futile efforts to fix things can cause us to erase the other 99% of our life that happened outside of the moments it took to hurt someone and the 100% of life we've yet to experience. If you're truly remorseful about your actions, God will not waste your ability to lead a family and be an example of what he's capable of for a man with a truly repentant heart, one way or the other. Yes, this same concept applies when it's the woman who has done the hurting and is now struggling to survive the aftermath.

This isn't some rah-rah speech to amp you up in light of what you did that hurt your spouse. This is a reminder to do what's necessary to keep yourself in this fight. She may be numb to anything she's doing to you now, but it won't last forever. If she's getting the help she needs, the worst of her behavior shouldn't last more than two or three months at most. So, you must keep going.

Secondly, it's time to fill your schedule with things that will elevate you and your wife out of this rut, starting with yourself. This is undoubtedly one of the hardest things to do, since all you want to do is fix the bond that was broken between you and your wife.

This is similar to our earlier discussion on how work must accompany faith, but this time, let's understand the importance of priority. Instead of working hard to get back to what you had before with your wife, which by the way, is normal, you need to pry your focus off of you two and completely immerse your attention in every crevice of your lowest self. Why? Because that's the version of you that hurt her.

Unless you have zero conscience about your wife's well-being, which you wouldn't be reading this if you didn't, then it's highly unlikely that you were your best self when causing her to look at you like a monster. So with that, you have a bone to pick with the version of you that did. The one that's depressed, has anxiety, has abandonment issues, can't handle rejection, can't control anger, is addicted to drugs and alcohol, or is dependent on something other than God for comfort.

What is wrong about that version of you? What is it looking for when tempted to make decisions that could ruin everything? Who has it not reconciled with from its childhood? What are the vices that it craves beyond your self-control's capacity to resist? How long does it take to manage and defeat the potential destruction your lowest self can cause?

These are the questions you need to find answers to. It's important that I re-emphasize from earlier in this book, that this is what needs to happen after you've completely gotten rooted in God, or it will serve as just more of your own understanding you're leaning on. No matter the upgrades you make to that, God has to be your new rock bottom, so that when you reach it, you land on the Rock, not the bottom. From that vantage point, you can now apply the rest of your understanding, keeping it aligned with God's will.

While you may think you're the only one who's fighting those battles that you lost before you made the decision to hurt your wife, humans have been around millions of years and there's nothing new under the sun.

God's saving grace in addition to the resources he's made available for this generation leave none of us with an excuse to remain the same, especially after hurting someone we claim to love. There is no justification to continue being your own primary or solo voice of reason about what corrective measures to take to avoid the mistakes you've made in the future. If you were qualified to be that voice of reason by yourself, you wouldn't be in this situation to begin with. Whatever pride or ego you have that's telling you, you can figure this out on your own, or that you know better than anyone else what's wrong with you is sure to make you repeat this cycle.

Lastly, now that you're aware that you need help from outside of your own self, and that self-pity won't save you, it's important to remember that your emotional high and corrective measures will take time to permanently change you from top to bottom. You will continuously be presented with opportunities to revert back to your old way of thinking and it's important that you leave no chances for regression.

I found that mere awareness can greatly reduce the chances for regression. A major shift in my growth came from becoming aware that in the most stressful times of my life, I would revert back to that default mindset of a single man that I had developed for years and foolishly allowed to go unchecked despite getting into a committed relationship. That meant whenever I was upset with the one that was in front of me, which of course, was my girlfriend and eventually my wife once I married her, my mind would immediately turn its attention towards what else was out there and making itself available.

Why?

Because in my singleness, that was what I became accustomed to, and I hadn't shaken that mentality before getting into a relationship.

That's not to say that singleness is bad because it's not. If you are dating one woman, and she's showing zero interest for two or three days in a row, it's completely fine for you to shift your attention to another woman who's reciprocating interest more effectively.

If one woman that you're dating is unavailable two or three weekends in a row for time to hang out and have fun, then there's nothing wrong with trying to see another woman the following weekend. If one woman does not understand the importance of speaking positively to and about you, then it makes sense for you to go out and speak to someone else who already understands the importance of that.

But in a marriage, especially one that has suffered a near-death blow by you, that single-minded mentality can be the final uppercut. If your woman is beginning to shift into 3-D behavior mode, you would be foolish to start getting any of that attention from outside the marriage. But if that's all you know, that's the most likely survival mechanism of the painful process of changing from the inside-out while having everything you love hanging in the balance. However, if you're at least aware, you stand a fighting chance to simply do the opposite of what's most familiar to you until you get to the point where your new way of thinking is now your default.

While we've discussed the different ways you may allow yourself to be vulnerable to an outside influence, don't get fooled into thinking the enemy is strictly outside looking to get in. Many times, the enemy is already inside and going to torment you so much with hypothetical scenarios, overthinking, and insecure conclusions you draw about your woman's behavior you go out and do something destructive just to distract you from those thoughts. I've seen countless men in my inbox suffering from their own misconceptions that eat at them in these times. Here are a few:

Misconceptions of a Healing Wife

<u>Misconception:</u> "She refuses to move on."

<u>Truth:</u> She's not refusing to move on. The effects of what you did to her just haven't moved on from her. While she may not be handling the emotions of this particular space with perfection, she never got the chance to prepare for what she'd do while in it because you promised that you would never put her there. You forced her to figure it out on the go. The least you could do is have patience.

<u>Misconception:</u> "She doesn't understand that I never meant to hurt her."

<u>Truth:</u> Her mind can't separate what you "mean" from what you won't do anymore. The problem isn't her inability to understand, it's your inability to match your promises with your actions.

Misconception: "She forgets that she's not perfect either."

Truth: She never lost sight of that. She just knows her imperfection didn't make her deserving of you breaking her. But if you felt like it was justification, then you should have said that in the beginning so she could have saved you both the trouble of waiting for her to heal from your lies.

Misconception: "I know I made a mistake, but I'm still a good man."

Truth: She's not hurting based on you being good or bad, she's hurting based on your decision-making being good or bad. Her heart is only as safe as the "mistakes" you keep yourself making, and right now, your heart represents danger regardless of how "good" you think you are.

Misconception: "All she had to do was say that if that's how she felt instead of acting all passive aggressive."

Truth: Through experience she's learned to regret telling you exactly how she feels because you don't know nor seemingly care to know how to make her feel comfortable telling you how she feels.

If your wife has developed a pattern of hiding her true feelings from you until some big blow-up, you luckily guess based on her passive-aggressive behavior, or you get a third party involved, she may have valid reason behind her actions. While the truth is, she has not been forthcoming about the way she feels, this doesn't exactly fall into the same file as dishonesty. Again, this is likely a reaction of one of the eight reasons you can find on the next page.

8 Reasons She Doesn't Feel Comfortable Sharing Her True Feelings With You

1. You don't listen to understand her. You only listen to gather enough details to help you prove to her why what she's feeling is invalid.
2. You don't make the effort to remember what she tells you after the conversation ends.
3. When she tells you how she feels, you act like you have more important things to do by the way you split your attention between her and your phone or laptop, checking out of the conversation once it starts getting inconvenient for you to continue listening, or missing the scheduled time to have the talk about her feelings altogether.
4. She told you something extremely personal, and you went and told someone else outside of the relationship without her permission.
5. You turn everything into either a joke or an opportunity to segue into sex including her moments of vulnerability where she just expressed her deepest feelings.
6. You take what she says, twist around, and later use it to attack or judge her.
7. When her feelings are something that offends you, you play dumb like you don't understand despite knowing full well that you do.
8. At best, you convey a thorough understanding of what she's told you, but there're never any actions that follow, which shows that you don't take her

seriously and she doesn't want to waste her breath anymore.

If any of the above apply to you, you have some work to do. If most of the above applies to you, you have a lot of work, plus apologizing, plus thanking God that somehow she still loves you.

For every wall that you built around your wife's heart with any of the above listed actions that kept her from relaying to you her innermost feelings, you decreased her trust in you, diluted her respect for you, and allowed whatever issue that came up next to hurt her ten times more. I'm not telling you this to persecute you, but if you feel a strong conviction as you read this, understand it's not meant to make you feel low or worthless. It's the feeling of the wool over your eyes finally being removed so you can see how much your wife loves you to still give you a chance even after years of not allowing her to feel comfortable putting her heart in your hands.

Hopefully, you will also see that a lot of your wife's behavior may feel like retaliation, vengefulness, or hatred, but it's actually a byproduct of being hurt. So, no, she's not a narcissist or finally showing her true colors. She may simply not know the exact words to articulate it, but rest assured that most, if not all, of the things she's done to deeply hurt you have either been caused or exasperated by your behavior with her.

Resist the temptation to justify your actions with any type of logic or nullify the impact of your actions by pointing out some undeniable flaw of hers. You are the leader, and that goes beyond just having the designation of making decisions in the house or getting the big piece of chicken for dinner.

You are also called to be a leader emotionally in setting the standard for the way you two are to deal with each other. Now, if she doesn't immediately follow your lead, that could either be a byproduct of how much trust she's still rebuilding in you or something else that she needs to deal with individually. However, your responsibilities as a leader do not change or shift based on her behavior. As men, we would be hypocrites to tout how we are not nearly as emotionally driven as women, yet use the emotional reaction they're driven by as a free pass to drop our standards.

Most of the battle at this point for you is going to be mental and spiritual. Just like any mental and spiritual battle, you have your part, and you must rely on God to do the His, which He's willing to. The best way to rely on God in this instance is to pray a prayer of grace over your wife. Instead of asking Him to teach her a lesson or forgive you for how you're going to choose to respond to her out of your anger, ask God to forgive her for what you believe she's done to hurt you. This will not only invite God in to do His part, but also posture your heart so you can do yours.

A prayer of grace over your wife isn't just for times like these. I personally pray this type of prayer any time a perceived wrongdoing from my wife is beginning to drive a wedge between us, and the results have been incredible. What normally would snowball for weeks or even months of tension over something minor(or major) will either be resolved quickly, or there's a heart posture of compassion for her point of view I couldn't achieve on my own. Either way, a prayer of grace for our wives accelerates the restoration of peace, oneness, and understanding much quicker than the lingering anger, frustration, or just trying to "explain" our point of view.

There's no specific formula to this prayer, but here's one similar to what I use that may be helpful for you:

A Prayer of Grace for Your Wife

Dear Heavenly Father,
I come to you on behalf of my wife,(say her name here), asking that you give her grace. She has hurt me deeply with her words and even her actions. She has offended me, shamed me, and cut me like never before, but I submit this pain to you to release me from and I submit her to you to forgive and heal. Give me a heart capable of the compassion that you have had for me when I've grieved you with my transgressions. Forgive her and wrap your loving arms around her in a way that only you can. Cover her from the torment she may be experiencing in response to the ways I and others have hurt her before & remove the scales of resentment from her eyes so she can see the love I truly have for her. Bless her with peace of mind. Protect her from her own consequences of her anger. Give me deeper insight into what she's feeling so that I'm not deceived by my own misperception. Sustain me. Have mercy on her. Reconnect us.

As the head of our household, I declare that we will no longer fall for the enemy's tricks to pit us against each other but will walk by faith that oneness with each other is already ours according to your perfect will. Thank you, Lord that it is done, in Jesus' name. Amen.

Again, this is a spiritual battle, first and foremost. You, I, nor any man is strong enough to do this on our own, so I recommend that in addition to doing all that you can do, also relying on God. Get vulnerable with Him. Cry. Yell. Whatever you must do to let him have every bit of what you're going through, do it. He WILL help you, and you will notice your strength and her softness increase, dramatically.

Note to the healing spouse: This tends to be the more frustrating portion of the process for healing spouses who are in the anger stage of grieving. To those of you who are not, you may find yourself in this position and not realize it until afterwards. Either way, the anger is normal. Defensiveness is normal. Doing everything you can to remind the one who hurt you that he's hurt the wrong one is also normal. I get it.

However, this fire that's breathing out from your actions will consume both the one you're aiming at and yourself as well. I'm not fond of even the slightest hint of victim blaming or shaming, so that's not what this is. It's just the truth, and I've seen it happen countless times. Children get caught in it. Credit scores get caught in it. Friendships are ruined. The price of acting or speaking out of anger is so much higher than what you get in return, and in the end, it elongates the time for your recovery despite its temporary soothing.

You end up staying in fight, flight, or freeze mode, in this case fight mode, which keeps your internal state responding to your spouse as if there's a life-or-death emergency. Comfort won't come from seeing your spouse crucified every day, but rather from seeing your spouse as your healer. Of course, this doesn't mean he can solely heal you, but if he's doing the right things, that's the role he's playing and your feeling of safety will come when you allow him to play that role for you.

With that, remember that you don't owe your spouse access to you 24/7. If you feel your anger rising to what could be an unsafe level, it's okay to let him know and step away for a few hours, maybe even a full twenty-four hours while you let the dust settle before coming back to deal with an issue.

Typically, anger responses convince us they'll make us feel so much better than what they actually will. Giving grace in place of the anger can feel like even more of an injustice for the spouse who's already getting off easy for what he's done to you, but that's your broken heart speaking. It's scared to let your guard down and would rather unload the magazine clip instead. However, remember that you have control over it. The shortness of breath, rising temperature, increased heart rate, and even adrenaline will subside if you train it to, and you can't train it to by continuing to let it dictate your reactions.

Chapter 5

She Can't Love a Man She Doesn't Feel Safe With

"So, he thinks he can just butter me up and everything will go back to normal?"
"He must think I'm stupid."
"I'm not falling for this again."
"He's only doing all this because he got caught."
"Why should he get what he wants from me while I'm still over here suffering?"

As a healing spouse, you may have thoughts like this running across your mind. Please understand something; it's normal. However, they're not helpful, unless your husband isn't genuinely looking to be your ally in your healing.

"Well, how do I know that he's genuinely different from the version of himself or original person who hurt me?"

Here's a quick list of signs your husband is a man helping your healing, not adding to your need to heal.

- Actions to prove he's remorseful for his part in your pain are consistent despite his emotional ups and downs. Typically, a decision to hurt you stemmed from an emotional mismanagement on his part, and a man whose character fluctuates with his emotions is still unsafe to love.

- There's a general receptiveness to the third party or external guidance you two have agreed to turn to. He's not sticking to doing everything "his way," but instead, is willing to try new ways of being by your side through this time. People who don't change typically are stuck in their own rigid way of thinking.

- He has made tangible sacrifices to focus on your needs and has made space in his life to continue those sacrifices going forward. This may look like money he no longer spends on recreation or new shoes, but instead is investing in more help with supporting you two in healing your marriage. It may even look like a sleep schedule he changes to make sure he can help around the house before or after work. You know what things he holds important to him. See if he's been willing to shift anything about how he does those things to create an opportunity to be more present for your expressed needs.

- There's tangible evidence of a personal conviction about the man he can no longer be. This looks like boundaries he's setting and new habits he's creating that you didn't have to "pressure" him into, but rather he came up with in an effort to be a better man. If it's not personal to him, it won't last.

- He accepts accountability, not resists it. He welcomes new ways to measure his commitment to his promises even if it means bringing someone else into his business more than he's ever been comfortable with. People who aren't truly ready to change hate accountability.

- He's compassionate in times you're cruel to him. This is a tricky one because your cruelty needs to end, but his compassionate response is an indicator that he understands why you're currently acting that way. While defensiveness is natural to some extent, compassion in times where he could "return fire" is a reflection of how much time he's quietly dwelled on the depth of your pain, which then creates compassion for that pain.

- There's an openness to learning, directly from you, more about why you feel the way you feel. Instead of cutting you off, dividing his attention with his phone or tuning you out, he will both quietly listen and confirm that what he received from what you said is accurate. This is a reflection of humility that he's aware he doesn't know everything, as well as his effort to not let that be an excuse to remain ignorant.

- His commitment to be better is not based on his own strength and might, but on God's Holy Spirit. Does this mean that in order to be an ally to your healing, your man has to turn water into wine? No. He's not perfect nor will he ever be. There will be mistakes. There will remain imperfections. Yet, a man who's truly repentant will dive deeper into his relationship with God, understanding that if his new changes are to be permanent, they will have to take place from the spiritual level on out. Some people have different beliefs, and that's fine, but I've seen and experienced the truth for myself, so ignore this point at your own risk. But when a man is in complete surrender to God, forsaking anything that's not of God, his heart and mind gets renewed better than ever.

Any mindset that he's got enough self-control and conviction on his own is either a byproduct of his emotion or arrogance and will eventually lead him back to his old ways. So, in this, it's important that you don't measure his relationship by whether or not you spot a flaw, because you will always find those. Rather, look for commitment to prayer, him studying the word of God, and measuring things according to the Bible instead of his own reasoning and logic.

These things are indicators that you're dealing with a man who is or is at least becoming the true ally to your healing, but I want to be clear; this does NOT mean he won't hurt you again. Good people make bad decisions all the time. I'm not making an excuse for his potential behavior. I want you to look deeper than just whether or not he's a good person, although that matters, a lot. But what also matters is whether or not he's going to make good or bad judgment calls that will affect the well-being of your heart.

There are drivers with perfectly clean driving records who've perished in car wrecks due to a momentary lapse in focus on the road. I've seen many teenagers with a bright future have their entire lives derailed because of a decision to try drugs just once. I've also seen a countless number of normally faithful people who shattered the one they loved because of a decision to step out on the relationship.

Generally speaking, these people all had the "character" we'd agree aligns with their end goal, so what was it that went into the out-of-character decision to lose everything?

Those were the small decisions long before the biggest deciding moment came. What prevents those small decisions from being the building blocks to destruction?

Boundaries.

The driver with a perfectly clean driving record may have driven the speed limit and worn their seatbelt at all times, but because he never set boundaries on when to change the music selection and when not to, he still suffered the same devastating end result as a wreckless driver. The teen with a bright future earned good grades and was active in the community, but because she never set boundaries on what kind of friends she should stay away from, she became complicit in their recreation, which were new drugs everyone else was doing, just like the "bad" kids.

The same thing goes for relationships. Being hurt by a man doesn't require him to be a bad person, first, nor does being good prevent him from doing bad things. No matter the character, there needs to be a clear understanding and consistent respect of boundaries to effectively shape behavior.

Some confuse this as meaning that they must eliminate all opportunities for the betraying partner to violate the commitment, which is only partly true.

Betrayal does not result from the presence of an opportunity to betray, but rather the absence of respected boundaries that would prevent betrayal.

There will always be other women. There will always be porn sites. There will always be social gatherings with other women, hyper-sexual Instagram accounts available, or women who walk by with nice bodies.

Trying to create a world where these things don't exist is pointless, but creating a relationship where boundaries on these things do exist is wise.

If you're going to place your confidence in anything, place it on that. "How do I know he's not going to do it again?" is all in the boundaries he respects, daily. Not in his level of emotion he expresses that he's deeply sorry and will never hurt you again. Not in his laundry list of qualifiers that prove he's a really good man. Not in his confessions to you or to the world so that now he's not living a lie. Not in your ability to punish him so severely with revenge that he knows next time that you're not the one, two, or the three. Definitely not in a bubble he needs to live in apart from society.

Respected boundaries are the only things you can have confidence in that you will not be hurt again. Blurred lines of boundaries are evidence that your heart is on the chopping block. It's that simple.

For boundaries to be respected, they must be expressed. Ideally, this is done before even the relationship, much less the marriage, but it's never too late to include them and in fact, is something that will continue to evolve as time goes on anyway.

But for those of you who have been hurt and decide that you will try to suffocate your partner's opportunities to hurt you in an effort to feel safe, again, you are trying in vain.

I get it. You cannot be blindsided and crushed like you once were. That's a completely understandable position. However, before you know that you're being betrayed, you'll know that boundaries are being blurred or even blatantly crossed. Treat them as the warnings they are. Don't shrug them off or stay silent. Don't beg or turn over the dinner table, no matter how tempted you are. Assertively communicate, and then act if they continue being disregarded.

The evidence that he won't hurt you again will show in the things he nips in the bud. He doesn't have to cut off all women, but if there's a pre-existing sexual relationship, he will nip in the bud any ability of that woman to contact him again, at least without your knowing of every detail beforehand and throughout. If there's never been a romantic relationship, he will nip in the bud any personal conversation, secrecy, or flirtation with her.

He shouldn't have to delete his social media, but if women are thirst trapping every other post, he will nip in the bud any involvement with their profiles. Not a follow, friend request, comment, "like", or personal message, whatsoever. If these women normally post respectful content but veer left, he should make sure his presence is NOT known on that post and that he removes her from his timeline if that type of content continues.

He shouldn't have to cut off his friends, but he will nip in the bud any activities a married man shouldn't be doing. That includes dancing with other women at clubs, even going to clubs, including strip clubs. If he shouldn't be on social media staring at half-naked women, why would it be okay for him to go to half-naked or fully naked women in person and stare at them in real life?

These are just some general boundaries I've seen be consistent in those men who effectively stop their hurtful end result before it can even start, but there are more. To truly build the confidence you need to feel safe, you need to know what boundaries you need to set and see that he respects them.

To get your list started, here are a few questions you can ask yourself.

- Have I told him what places I'm absolutely not comfortable with him going?
- Have I told him what women he currently communicates with that make me uncomfortable, and why it makes me uncomfortable?
- Have I told him what to do when he needs to come home late from work so that my mind doesn't wander?
- Have I told him how I truly feel about him watching porn? Has his answer placed my security as the priority, or his need to be in line with what's "normal" or what "should be" allowed for any man?
- Have we already established transparency across all mediums of communication (i.e., email, text, and social media access)?
- Has he ever broken down at least five key decisions that led to the one that hurt me and committed to what he's going to do to make those five key decisions differently? For example, if he sent a nude picture to another woman, he made the decision to first communicate with a woman he was sexually attracted to, exchange numbers with that woman,

keep their communication private, flirt with that woman, and not tell her about you…possibly. If he did tell her about you, then he allowed himself and her to disregard you, blatantly.

These questions give you infrastructure to start establishing boundaries that you can hold him accountable to. Notice, I did not say that you should be his mommy and try to raise him according to these standards, but hold him fully accountable as the adult that he is.

In frustration with the level of thought this can require, some will say, "Either he will or he won't_____(fill in the blank will hurtful action)." But for most out there, you know it's not that simple, and that's where the confusion lies. However, you don't have to be confused. Just be clear on whether or not he's prepared to hurt you or protect you.

If a person tells me they're going to wake up on time for work, I'm not going to primarily have confidence in the conviction in their voice or tears in their eyes when they're telling me. Neither will I have sole confidence in their good character.

I'm going to have confidence in what they do the night before to prepare their clothes, set their alarm, schedule upbeat music to play upon waking up, the time they shut off all electronics that could overstimulate their mind and prevent restful sleep, the wake-up calls they schedule from multiple accountability partners, and the bedtime that they honor.

Why? Because that's the necessary preparation, and preparation to make the right choice is much more meaningful than intentions to make the right choice. Stop guessing about his intentions and start assessing his preparation. That's how you get confidence on whether or not he will hurt you.

Here's another kicker.

A man can respect every boundary, evolve as a man, and defeat every demon that previously bound him to his most destructive ways, and it may still not be enough to make you feel safe.

Why? Because there's work you need to do as well.

"Why should I have to do anything when I'm not the one who messed up?"

If you thought something like that, I understand, and the truth is, it's not fair. When something isn't your fault, it shouldn't be any part of your responsibility to do anything to help fix it, but it is. Rejecting that responsibility isn't justice served, it's bitterness created.

When we get in a car wreck, the person who ran into you may be responsible for paying all the damage, but we still have to file a claim. We still have to notate the damages, and get the estimate done. If there was injury, they aren't going to go to the doctor for us. They're also not going to participate in the rehab. The person who caused damage on our vehicle has to pay for their mistake, but they can still only do so much no matter how at fault they are.

This is the same in a situation where someone else drove into your life and wrecked your heart. Whether he's willing to pay for the damage he caused or not, you have to show up for your part in creating the safety you need going forward.

I've stressed throughout this book how important it is for an ally to create safety, but it's null and void if the healing spouse isn't simultaneously ensuring internal safety.

Again, this isn't about making you responsible for what happened to you, but in realizing you're the deciding factor in what goes on in you.

The tortuous fears that you may get hurt again if you let your guard down are a result of remaining beliefs that it will happen. Beliefs are created by visual imagery, experiences, and strong emotion repeated over time. These beliefs can be emboldened or completely re-created by your external environment as well as your own thought patterns.

People who are successful tend to build and protect their beliefs around success to the point they cut off discouraging friends, block out depressing media, and speak often on success to repeat the thought patterns that yield their successful life.

Successfully healing and creating internal safety in your relationship will require the same thing. As a healing spouse, you've suffered an incredibly painful experience, and your thoughts will lean towards dwelling on it as a natural reaction to try and figure out ways to avoid it in the future. Even though you've now established that your current romantic environment is not the same one that hurt you, your mind won't immediately register that nor will it just happen over time.

This is where the "time heals all" perception has misled people. Time allows for either healing or normalizing the paranoia and high stress that comes with constantly expecting to be hurt again.

To make sure you don't fall into the latter category, you must begin a process I call *Challenging to Change*. This is where we question, counter, and replace the negative thought patterns with ones that are true to the reality of your new emotionally safe environment.

When you have a thought that elicits fear, anger, or pain, question it. For example,

Thought: "He must think I'm stupid."
Feeling: Anger

Your natural response will seek to bring soothing to this feeling of anger by teaching him a lesson that manifests as either a lashing out, shutting down, or other passive-aggressive behavior. However, a question of, "Is this thought rooted in the past experiences or current proof of what he thinks?" Another question is, "Is it possible that he has a different reason for what he's saying or doing that I may be unaware of?"

This type of questioning allows the separation of these thoughts from your immediate validation so they can have an opportunity to be evaluated and thrown out if they're not serving your goal of internal emotional safety. It won't be easy at first, but with practice, you will get better at it.

Once you question the thought, it's time to counter it with possibilities that produce the opposite of your unsafe emotion of anger. For example:

"Maybe he doesn't know the way he made me feel with what he just said."
"Maybe he's genuinely unaware of the best way to handle this, but trying his best, nonetheless."
"Maybe he's acting out of nerves or operating on a tired mind."

These are just general examples, but the point is to insert possibilities your mind won't voluntarily consider, possibilities that bring further separation between you and the current feeling of anger you have.

Next, assertively communicate the situation as you perceived it and what feelings that perception has created. However, make it clear that you want to know exactly what he meant by what it was he did or said.

If it is a situation where he has insulted your intelligence, it's okay to tell him that and then set a boundary that he'll be held accountable for. However, in most cases, you will realize that your emotions painted a completely different picture than that of reality, which is okay. It doesn't mean you're "crazy" or "insane," it just means your mind is still in protective mode, and you have work to do because you're no longer dealing with an attacker you must protect yourself from, but rather your ally who's also protecting you.

To fully change the thought, you must replace it. Do this by writing down your original thought, the negative emotion it produced, and then the reality that was contrary to your original thought. Title the list *Challenge to Change*.

This seems a bit tedious, but this is the work I referred to in the beginning of the book we must all do when we want change. Writing this down will allow you to collect a list of lies your emotions have tried to convince you of while showing your ability to now create the emotions you desire based on your reality.

This list will begin to restore the feeling of control you have over your internal environment that we all lose when we've been hurt. It will also begin to recondition your mind to start accepting the love and protection from your husband as the repetition of hearing his true intentions take precedence over the previous intentions that hurt you before.

The biggest indicator that you don't have safety in your relationship will be in the negative emotions you regularly feel as well as the events that create those emotions. Conversely, the biggest indicator of your safety returning are positive, peaceful, and encouraging emotions beginning to increase.

They can only increase with your permission, and will do so, abundantly, with your participation. It won't be easy, but you will find over time that it was more than worth it, and so are you.

Note to the ally: Your apologies are pointless without changed behavior.

What behavior needs to be changed? The small open doors that led to her trust being robbed. The seemingly insignificant blurred lines of respect to the relationship that erased all confidence in your ability to emotionally protect her.

Many times, you feel like your wife is not doing her part in the healing process when really, you're still playing the part of the one who hurt her. If that one who hurt her was you, then you know better than anyone what things hurt her. Find the root, uproot it, and reinsert something in its place that will position your wife to be the contributor to this healing process you desire. If you don't know where to start, let your complaints be the clues.

For instance:

Complaint: "She won't tell me what's wrong when I ask."

Possible root: You may be asking in the wrong way, tone, or at the wrong time for her. Maybe she's not comfortable with your verbiage. Maybe she'd feel more comfortable with this question being asked in front of a third party so they can help her articulate herself more effectively, or help you understand what she's saying. Maybe she feels like you're not listening because you're not showing proof that you are.

Changed behavior: Get help on understanding different communication styles. Tell her in advance you'd like to take this conversation to your trusted third party. Ask her to guide you on ways to make her more comfortable in difficult conversations. Practice the steps in this book on how to listen to understand.

Here's another example.

Complaint: "She's not giving me a chance to earn her trust."

Possible root: Those doors to other women haven't been closed. You defended the women who were complicit in your actions that hurt your wife, showing that you have their back more than you currently have hers. You still follow these women on Instagram, possibly out of fear that you will offend them. You haven't blocked their numbers in your phone, showing that you refuse to burn that bridge. You're still carrying on friendships with the opposite sex that you haven't brought your wife in on. You refuse to give your wife access to those lines of communication formally used to connect with other women. You're still going to nightclubs and strip clubs.

Changed behavior: Literally, the opposite of everything I just listed. Close the doors. Block or delete the women. Let your wife have access to everything. Yes, everything. Bring your wife in on friendships with the opposite sex, which honestly, should be limited if you're married.

Why? Because these innocent friendships and lines of communication are breeding grounds for betrayal. Many people maintain these breeding grounds because they're not guarantees of betrayal, but without very intentional boundaries, they're dangerous. I do believe friendships can transcend biology, but without boundaries, biology will eventually dominate the course of the "friendship" against the best interests of a marriage. This may cause a healing wife to resist giving her trust to her husband despite him no longer continuing on in the action that originally hurt her.

Studies show that 82% of infidelities of both men and women start off "innocent."

A lunch with several coworkers where there's a few side conversations with the opposite sex coworker sitting next to you that continues after work and creates comfort with sharing details on life at home. This comfort leads to a safe place where you and the coworker get attached because it feels like relief from respective relationship turmoil, and then the safe space becomes supplementation for what's missing in the form of an emotional affair. Now this coworker is a shoulder to lean on in times of distress, a ray of sunshine when you're discouraged, a listening ear when you need to vent. Because these are things you originally expected from your wife, but are now outsourcing from another woman, you're officially in an emotional affair.

A reply to a "Happy Birthday" text from a former flame that drifts into conversation about what you're doing to celebrate, then when the next time is that you'll be in town. You have no plans on being in town, but now that flame so happens to be coming in your city for a weekend and would love to see you for an "innocent" cup of coffee. This coffee outing goes on long enough to get hungry and she so happens to love the menu at the restaurant in her hotel so long as you're not "scared you'll get in trouble." Your ego takes over because "you're not a child," and you get to within walking distance of her hotel room. Finally, your flesh takes over and you end up in her bed.

A night at a club with the guys to have a few drinks that turns into you playing the wingman for your friend. This leads to entertaining a woman to keep her busy while your buddy makes moves on her friend, but to see it through, you have to go with him back to his place to "kick it" afterwards. This started off as something you were just doing for him, but as he's in the back room "scoring," it arouses both you and the friend you were originally just keeping busy to the point clothes are coming off.

A long-time friend-girl who knows about your wife but rarely speaks to her. You two have been friends since childhood, so it's cool. Except, one day she catches her boyfriend cheating. She gets angry and wants to get back at him and will do anything to see him bleed the way she's bleeding. She doesn't initially have the boldness to try you, sexually, so instead she just sends a few risqué pictures. Either you'll initiate the encounter, or she can fake-apologize for sending the pictures as if it was a mistake. Now, at best, you have sexual photos of another woman in your phone, and at worst, you take the bait and go all the way.

These are real scenarios and only a fraction of those I've seen play out where men with good initial intentions put themselves in position to fall victim to their carnal nature. However, do not mistake in thinking you're an actual victim. Right now, you have the opportunity to put measures in place to prevent them by removing all breeding grounds for betrayal and create a solid foundation for your wife's ability to trust you.

If you feel like she's not giving you a chance to earn more of her trust, it's likely because she still sees you playing Russian Roulette with the little you do have.

Chapter 6

The Illusion of Revenge

"How could she, of all people, do this to me?"

I was doing a one-on-one with Troy, a man who had been reaching out to me for weeks on each of my platforms to try and get on a call for help with handling his recent discovery of his wife's affair.

They had been married eight years, had three beautiful children, and were supposed to be starting a business together pretty soon. The first two years of the marriage were tumultuous and suffered a devastating blow where he'd gotten walked in on in the act of cheating by his then-pregnant wife.

She found it in her heart to forgive him, and truly forgave him, but a hole had been created in her that she didn't know how to close again. Her old perspective on life had been shattered and part of her had been changed forever.

She'd previously never given even the slightest hint that she could be attracted to another man, yet she found herself explaining to her husband of eight years that she had not only been cheating on him but had also dissolved their joint savings in an investment into her affair partner's new gym he'd be opening and would soon be having his baby.

Troy had no way of knowing about the money since she was in charge of that part of the family's operations. They had a nice system going. He would make the money; she would sort out where it went since she'd gotten her bachelor's in finance. She was able to hide her affair in the time she spent going to the gym since her affair partner was her personal trainer and married also.

Everything was running like clockwork in her extramarital relationship until she began falling in love with the trainer, trusting him enough to both invest in his business idea over the course of six months, but also in having consistent, unprotected sex.

This brought Troy to his knees, unable to make sense of it, since he'd done everything he promised he'd do since he'd put her in the same position. He'd stopped the affairs. He made other women respect boundaries. He got treatment for his addiction to pornography. He'd made many promises and kept them, yet that didn't stop her desire for revenge...so he thought.

While some would say this was rightful karma coming back around to him like clockwork, I wondered if it was deeper than just a typical revenge-cheating scenario. From everything he'd told me about Melissa and the amount of time that'd passed since her heart was broken, it didn't add up.

I requested for an individual call with her to help give me the full picture, and when she accepted, my suspicion was validated. Melissa wasn't exacting revenge, at least not in a traditional sense. She didn't make a conscious decision to make Troy pay for his mistakes or send a message to him.

She didn't even suspect that he was still carrying on in his habits of old.

But from the day she'd walked in on him in the act of cheating while she was carrying his child, the dynamic of the marriage shifted. She'd forgiven him, but couldn't ignore that on a daily basis, he was walking around emotionally unscathed while she was figuratively on a ventilator. She didn't feel that she needed to even the score, but in an effort to rebuild her self-esteem once the baby was born by getting in shape, she found herself relating to her personal trainer who was going through a similar experience.

Her overwhelming feelings of grief felt much safer in his hands than her husband's since she hadn't yet begun seeing her husband as her ally in her healing. He was still the "enemy." However, her personal trainer was the perfect substitute since he immediately came in as an ally. He was going to guide her into better self-esteem by pushing her to better physical health. He was a great listener, as it was a part of his job to evaluate the physical and psychological state of his clients to get them the best results. He was encouraging and motivating, as is typical of other fitness professionals. He was gentle, something she got to experience since there would be hands-on involvement of correcting her form. Long before this was sexual, it created a level of comfort with him that she would never allow with any other man outside her relationship.

Yet, in the most vulnerable season of her healing, this was a recipe for disaster. Whereas most healthily married couples would wisely discuss boundaries for such engagement, her husband carried too much guilt to dare speak on what she should not be able to do and she didn't respect him enough to care anyway. She'd forgiven him, but as we discussed, there's so much more required in order to receive closure, and without that closure, the door to her heart was wide open.

Again, she wasn't predisposed to cheating. She'd never taken such a thing lightly, even in light of being betrayed herself. She didn't think it was a righteous recourse for her husband's actions, but in a state of such pain, she inadvertently found soothing in the presence of her personal trainer, and over time experienced something similar to an amygdala hijack.

This was a term coined by psychologist Daniel Goleman in his 1995 book *Emotional Intelligence: Why It Can Matter More Than IQ*. In essence, an amygdala hijack is when the part of the brain that strictly responds to emotion can disable the frontal lobe's part of the brain that gives us the ability to think logically, rationally, and according to our morals.

While this amygdala hijack is sudden, I've witnessed the same phenomena play out over time after a traumatic experience, especially when there's a visual element added. Some spouses find out they're being cheated on by seeing mere evidence in the form of flirtatious texts; others may even see explicit pictures. In Melissa's case, she literally walked in and saw the penetration. She heard the sounds. She smelled the smells. She felt the undergarments of her husband's affair partner at her feet. At that point, she was made a perfect candidate of the amygdala hijack, and Troy is fortunate that it didn't play out much worse.

But it was difficult to appreciate that upon finding out his formerly pure, beloved wife was responsible for the same atrocity he had committed. He could only make sense of it by believing it to be revenge, but Melissa profusely denied that notion, which made it impossible for him to process and put to rest.

I didn't lecture him about how you reap what you sow. I didn't tell him that what goes around comes back around again. Instead, I explained to both of them why the Bible teaches us that the heart is deceiving (Jeremiah 17:9), and why psychology teaches us that this can happen to anyone when our frontal lobes are not in control.

Before anything could be repaired, they both needed to get on the same page and more importantly, the right page about what had happened and why.

Something a lot of men don't love to hear, but is the truth, is that being attracted to others outside of our current relationship is a human experience, not something exclusive to the morally corrupt. This means that our wives, no matter how innocent, self-controlled, and committed to the marriage they are, will be attracted to others while married to us. It's not always sexual. Sometimes our wives can be attracted to another man's intelligence, and therefore be drawn to more of his insight on a particular subject. Sometimes it'll be his kindness or humor that draws them into more of the content he creates online. It can even be the way that he loves his own wife, in which a wife will be drawn into seeing more displays of his love toward her.

Attraction is simply the evocation of interest, liking, or pleasure; it is not always sexual. In fact, many times it's not sexual in the beginning, but ends up evolving into that over time of the initial attraction being acted on. Because Melissa had never cheated a day in her life and wasn't promiscuous before meeting Troy, she let her guard down. She was caught slipping by her squeaky clean fidelity record, and like many, forgot that she's not an exception to the rule of attraction. Previous attractions to men had simply been guarded by her frontal lobes, unable to go past anything that would be inappropriate, and therefore went undetected.

However, this wasn't the same version of Melissa who could see an attractive man, shrug him off, and keep on moving. This wasn't the same Melissa that could hear a man speak kindly to her and have zero curiosity of what it must be like to get that on the regular without flashbacks of walking in on illicit sex. This wasn't the same Melissa that heard the painful stories of someone who had been deeply traumatized by betrayal but could not relate.

This version of Melissa was vulnerable, no longer the ethically invincible wife, but now the wife hanging on by a thread. Her personal trainer knew that and became the rope she could grab onto in all the wrong ways. His compassionate words when he countered her negative self-talk with uplifting reminders felt like a much-needed hug. This hug was something her husband was trying to give her, but to Melissa, the sting was too real and threatening that if she "fell" for it, she'd just be hurt again. Troy's uplifting words had taken on an identity of simply trying to clean up his mess and avert consequences, so she resisted, while her personal trainer quietly picked up the mantle.

The trainer began giving Melissa relationship advice in addition to the physical guidance, and this caused her to idealize him as "getting it," in all the ways her husband didn't. Again, she wasn't evaluating from her morals or rational thought, but rather her amygdala that latched on to the hint of safety we all find in being related to.

The problem is, when she did this, her subconscious mind hadn't separated her personal trainer's perception from his reality. Not because he was intentionally deceiving her, but because she only saw a fraction of him. This was the part he was okay with letting outsiders see, and she was indeed an outsider, no matter how comfortable she personally felt letting him in. She still didn't know his good, bad, and ugly like she knew Troy's. She only knew the surface layer, which was, of course, eons better than Troy's deepest, darkest layers. With that, she subconsciously placed her trainer on a pedestal her husband would never reach.

Over time, Melissa would be triggered at home with Troy and find refuge at the gym, which meant finding refuge in the comfort of her personal trainer. Her love for working out simultaneously grew with her love for him, something neither of them had realized until it was too late. Like a frog in a pan of water slowly heating to eventually burn it alive, Melissa and her now emotional affair partner escalated into full on sexual intercourse once he got a promotion to director at the gym she was working out at. This provided opportunities for privacy in his top floor office during their normal gym time, and with Troy at home simply happy to have not lost his wife, he didn't have the slightest clue. That was, until she was three months pregnant and now fearing for her life since her affair partner's wife, whom he told her he'd divorced, was now seeking Melissa's blood.

Melissa couldn't believe the mess she'd created and was equally as disheveled as Troy since she was both the betrayer and betrayed at the same time.

When I listened to her speak through a flood of tears, I didn't sense an evil human being with no conscience, or even a scorned woman who'd finally exacted justice on her husband. I saw a woman who had gotten what most would consider the sweet taste of revenge, but realized it was actually bitter and poisonous. She didn't ingest this poison on purpose, but rather by the common route of "I'm not that kind of person, so I don't have to worry about that."

"It's no big deal."
"I'm not the one who needs boundaries, he is."
"I'm not the one who can't control their genitals."
"He's just insecure because he's scared he's going to taste his own medicine."

After interviewing dozens of women in the same position as Melissa, I realized they all held similar beliefs before stepping on to their slippery slope of revenge-cheating. It wasn't intentional or premeditated. It just "happened." They were vulnerable. It wasn't even in their character.

They also all had similar thoughts after the experience.

"It wasn't worth it."
"If I could go back and do it again, I'd just leave."
"I'd give anything to take it back."

"It made me feel like a piece of meat."

The feeling of being used that the original betrayal produced wasn't cancelled out, but exponentially increased. They realized the affair partner saw them as easy prey, not someone they really cared about. Some even say it seemed to justify the original betrayal as opposed to correcting what went wrong from it.

I say this because in the process of healing together without hurting each other, we must be careful not to do things that will hurt ourselves. While most see revenge-cheating as a conscious decision, the end result is the same if you take the betrayal you've experienced and double it due to a lack of discernment in a time of vulnerability.

Being careful not to go down this road is not a matter of protecting your betraying spouse, but rather a matter of protecting yourself from additional wounds being added to those already there.

There are two groups of women I've seen who have slightly different experiences.

1. Previously promiscuous women
2. Women who are still in the anger stage of their grieving process

If you are neither of these, you will experience 100% of the drawbacks of allowing opportunistic intruders into your heart and/or body post-relationship trauma. However, those two women, like the rest of you, are not exempt to the spiritual ramifications.

The spiritual exchange of sexual intercourse is real. Soul ties are real. It's the reason why your life can be going fine but the moment you start a sexual relationship with someone, you notice your life going downhill. Things begin getting shaky at your job. You can't get as much sleep as you used to, or you begin having nightmares. All of a sudden there's drama in your friendships. Things pop up on your credit score that don't make sense. Opportunities begin to fall apart right at the edge of your breakthrough. Your energy seems to dwindle a lot earlier in the day than before. You can't focus like you once could.

The list goes on.

Some people think this is because of different natural-world causes, which could be in some cases. But in many, it has a lot to do with the change in their spiritual environment, which is often affected by those you're spiritually engaging or have engaged with.

That's why sex is never casual. Yes, we eventually catch feelings, but we also catch spirits. The Bible speaks about this in 1 Corinthians 6:16 when it states that if a man (or woman) sleeps with a prostitute, that person has become one with that prostitute. Any time the Bible speaks of becoming one, it's not literally speaking that two people fuse into one walking, talking human being, but that there's now been a spiritual contract established between the two, thus giving passageway of each other's spirit(s) to flow one to the other.

Have you ever noticed that a person you've slept with randomly pops up on your mind after years of not seeing or hearing from them? Have they randomly reached out to you at just the moment you were thinking of them? That's evidence that a spiritual contract is still in place between the two of you, a.k.a., a soul tie, which means other spirits they had at the time you two engaged are likely present as well.

These soul ties require repentance, prayer, and fasting to break off once and for all, so if you have them, there is hope. But there is also a responsibility, no matter how heartbroken we may be by our spouse, to protect our bodies, hearts, and spirit.

Intramarital healing is in alignment with that mission, but our outside behavior during the process is just as important. We must make sure that in the wise effort to raise the standard on our spouse that we don't inadvertently drop the standards for ourselves. If teaching your spouse a lesson requires that to take place, that spouse should have no place in your life.

Removal is so much better than revenge. In the dating phase, the removal was of the person. If a new prospect showed a red flag, you removed them. If he disrespected you, disrespected your time, or got "too busy" all of a sudden, you showed him to the exit. Removal is a healthy response to those things, but in marriage, the removal may be of yourself in certain aspects.

Removal of sex. Removal of cuddling. Removal of emotional connection. Again, this isn't like the dating phase where the removal is permanent, but some things need to be put on a shelf while more important matters are dealt with.

If there's a crack in the floor, you don't fix it with furniture still sitting on top. You remove the furniture, put it somewhere else, and then you deal with the crack in the floor. The floor is the foundation. The furniture and nice décor will be there to enjoy later, but it won't be enjoyable if the floor is cracked.

If your "floor" is cracked in your relationship, move the furniture to another room, not someone else's home. They'll just put their feet on your couch and break the china. If the floor can't be repaired, then it's okay to move out, for good. Otherwise, keep things in house if you want the sanctity to return.

Chapter 7

Egos Are For Kids

"When I was a child, I spake as a child, I understood as a child, I thought as a child: but when I became a man, I put away childish things" 1 Corinthians 13:11 KJV

Before I got married, I was inundated with the statistics of how many marriages end in divorce, in which, the last time I checked, that was about half, and most of those ended within the first two years. I found myself wondering why, so I researched and found that studies show the most common reasons are money issues, infidelity, and thinking a ring will solve deep-seated issues, which it does not.

After digging deeper, I found the common denominator in struggling marriages--ego.
Webster's Dictionary defines the ego as one of the three divisions of the psyche in psychoanalytic theory that serves as the organized conscious mediator between the person and reality especially by functioning both in the perception of and adaptation to reality.

Don't worry, if you didn't get all of that. The context of ego I'm going to speak to is more along the lines of the thing that makes a person egotistical. This means he or she is vain, boastful, indifferent to the well-being of others, selfish, and has an over-inflated sense a self-confidence.

Women are not just these perfect angels who can do no wrong, but again, as society has raised many men to identify our masculinity synonymously with what should be recognized as ego, we tend to suffer from this the most. Suffering from this and never checking it can poison an otherwise healing environment for our wives and healthy relationship in general.

I've noticed that for men who have successfully contributed to a healing environment for their wife and therefore made it over that two-year threshold, ego is one of the very first things they realized must die. When I asked questions about what that looked like, most of them simply described it as "growing up," and now, I can't unsee the connection between ego and being stuck in a childish mentality.

In the movie *The Lion King*, Simba and Nala's youth was captured perfectly when they made the decision to leave Pride Rock and go to the hyenas' territory. Although they were forbidden to do so, their childlike naivety and especially Simba's ego motivated their decision to go anyway in which they quickly found out why they were told to never go there, and they only made it out safely because unexpected help arrived.

Similarly, when two children are fussing, and you ask either of them what's going on, you can expect that whatever you hear is going to be a one-sided point of view along the lines of, "He took my toy!"

Of course, we wouldn't look at these things and say that a child is egotistical. We would simply say that a child is being a child. But when we see the same qualities in what should be an adult, that's when it becomes ego, which are childlike tendencies hidden behind an adult exterior and maintained by foolish pride.

For many, this works on the dating scene because there is no need for maturity unless you are courting for marriage. But, the worldly view of dating allows for one to treat each person you come across as a new toy. Similar to how a child treats a new toy, in dating, once it's no longer new to you, you can simply move on to the next toy. You also don't have to consider anything outside of your point of view. You can simply sift through a multitude of people until you find someone who on the surface level either thinks like you or is willing to concede to your point of view since neither of you are emotionally invested.

This is why people who love dating or have a long history of serial dating with no intention for marriage typically have a hard time adjusting to marriage or even a serious relationship. Why? Because marriage is a grown man and woman territory.

There is no moving on to a new "toy" when yours doesn't feel so new anymore. Even after noticing a defect, or being the cause of a particular defect, marriage requires us to either assist in fixing the toy or find new ways to love this toy in lieu of its defects.

I spoke recently to an old buddy of mine from college, trying to help him decide what to do at a crossroad in his relationship, but his ego made it difficult for him to understand this. He had been with his girlfriend for a little over a year, and she'd begun bringing up the subject of marriage. He resisted the notion of marriage, being that it would require him to commit to her despite whatever "defects" presented themselves on down the road.

He said to me, "What if she gains weight? What if she gets complacent? What if I meet somebody else on down the road that I like more? What if one day I just wake up and don't want her anymore and simply want to be alone? Marriage complicates things and I don't think it's worth it."

While he couldn't see it for himself, it was plain as day that his ego was hiding behind these questions and masquerading as intellectual forethought. I'm not saying that a person is still a child mentally if they are not interested in marriage, but the reasons he gave all point to the fact he had yet to grow up. It was confirmed when I asked him what kept him in the relationship this long. His answer, "She rides for me. She loves me for me, good and the bad, and I know she ain't goin' nowhere."

When he said that, I laughed out loud to keep my initial facial expression from offending him. At that moment, it became clear that his ego was not only too big to allow him to get married, but mirrors the same ego that would ruin his marriage if he did choose to marry.

I asked him, "Well, what if you lose your hairline?" "What if you get inconsistent?" "What if her ex gets his act together and comes back looking for another shot?" "What if she wakes up one day and realizes she'd be just fine without you?"

As expected, he got defensive, but I continued on anyway explaining that marriage didn't complicate things. His egotistical vantage point of readily receiving the very thing he refused to give or protect with a long-term commitment is what complicated things. Without his ego, he'd be able to respect where she was coming from in wanting evidence that they were both ready to give each other what they were expecting from the other. He was reluctant to give her the same confidence in him that he had in her of her love for him despite his "defects."

Him not yet marrying her was actually a gift to her for the time being, because if he did he would have either had to face the challenge of killing his ego or suffer the fate of killing his marriage, and it likely wouldn't have taken him long to do that.

Of course, the goal of marriage isn't simply to not get a divorce, but to be able to allow that marriage to add value to your life as well as your spouse's. When dealing with a marriage that needs healing, we are dealing with a marriage that's providing little to no value due to the consuming damage that's been done on at least one of the spouses. If your spouse has suffered in your marriage, she has to relearn to love and trust you all over again and will never do so with an unchecked ego.

Don't get me wrong, there are marriages that last several decades where the ego is present, but I've never seen one where both the husband and wife are getting anything close to the most out of their marriage. In fact, these tend to be the types of marriages that seem more like two people who are serving a sentence than two people who are pushing each other both towards their purpose in life and enjoying every step of the journey.

While some wives somehow stomach a man's undying ego for a large portion of the relationship, there are certain types of wives who will not. If any of the following characteristics on the next page describes your wife, then she is the type who will not tolerate ego for long.

Character Traits of a Woman Who Will NOT Tolerate an Egotistical Man

1. She's aware of the value she brings you and others around her.
2. She's committed to achieving her individual purpose assigned by God.
3. She doesn't tolerate disrespect.
4. She doesn't reward your wrongdoing with continued access to her.
5. She's able to acknowledge when she's wrong.
6. She has a strong support system outside of you.
7. She has a life outside of you.
8. While she values marital commitment, it's emotional and spiritual commitment within the marriage that she values most.
9. She's not afraid to express her disappointment when you don't keep your word.
10. She values your contribution but would find a way to survive if you left her no other choice.

The more characteristics from this list that directly relate to your wife, the more dysfunction is likely a byproduct of your ego as well as the shorter the time window you have to find a way to kill it.

So, let's go through a few situations and look at what it means to not have ego versus what would be an ego.

You work every day because you're the breadwinner of the house. You come home from work about two hours before bedtime. Your wife asked you for at least one of those hours to be spent strictly with her. However, it's the playoffs and there's a game on every night that you get home just in time to watch.

An egotistical approach to your wife's request would be to remind her how you're the breadwinner, and your time after work is yours to spend how you want to, and if she likes having all the bills paid, then she needs to allow you to decompress how you want. This would likely discourage your wife from bringing any requests to you and result in her being detached in the near future before eventually questioning if this is the right marriage for her.

Conversely, a non-egotistical approach would be to consider your wife's request and the unmet need that's motivating her request, Then, measure the importance of your wife's unmet need versus your desire to catch the playoffs every night. The lack of ego makes way for the wise consideration that your life will be easier without witnessing every minute of the playoffs versus living with a woman who has a need that's not being met.

That doesn't mean that you can't enjoy a basketball game every now and then, but it does mean that you must keep things in priority if you can only have one or the other relative to your wife's need for quality time with you. So, instead of watching the playoffs every night that you get home from work, your wife would probably appreciate if you dedicated a few nights after work to spending time with her and even an agreement to make time on your day off.

Or let's say your wife expresses to you that she'd appreciate if you woke the children up some days and got them ready for school so that she could sleep in. However, before getting married, you two decided that you would be the protector and provider and she would be the homemaker, which included primary responsibility over the children.

An egotistical response is to tell her that if she expects you to start doing more of her job, then it's time for her to get a job and start putting food on the table. This approach is sure to show your wife that you have not given a second thought to why she's made such a request and how it can be beneficial not only to her but also to you and your children in the long-term. A non-egotistical approach would be to offer to your wife that you would try this one to two days a week before writing it off as something you won't do. Although you may initially be reluctant to take on an additional responsibility, an honest effort to try her suggestion shows that her perspective is valid even if you don't initially agree.

Let's look at one more. Your wife expresses to you that your habit of watching pornography makes her uncomfortable and makes her question if she'll ever be able to sexually satisfy you. An egotistical response would be that it's perfectly normal for men to watch porn and that if you're not out sleeping with anybody else, then it shouldn't be a problem. The reason why this is egotistical is because your consideration stops at the surface level of the challenge to something you believe should be permissible instead of removing that first line of egotistical defense so you could penetrate to the real root of why your wife is concerned about the fact that you watch porn.

A non-egotistical approach would be to thank your wife for having the courage to express to you what her issue is despite knowing that this is a normality for most men. Next, follow with an admittance to this being something you were not considerate of how it would make her feel. Lastly, based on your decision that pornography is less important to you than your wife's security, commit to completely ending any consumption of pornography.

As you can see, the number-one difference between an egotistical response or approach and a non-egotistical one is ignoring that initial impulse to be right. Yes, I'm re-emphasizing an earlier point because it is that important. When you ignore that initial impulse to be right, you dramatically increase your chances for being connected, even if you don't concede 100% to your wife's request. At absolute minimum, the fact that you would even take a non-egotistical approach would likely result in your wife feeling safe as well as growing respect for you in the marriage.

Over time, consistently killing your ego will show you how foolish it is that most men believe that having an ego and being a real man go hand-in-hand. So long as you have an ego, you will always have to fight to prove that you are a man. Why? Because it won't be evident in how you carry yourself.

If it's still not clear to you whether or not you've been egotistical in dealing with your wife, her disposition lately could give you some evidence of that. Of course, you can outright just ask her, "Hey honey, do you feel like I've been egotistical in any of our dealings over the past six months?" I guarantee you that if you have, she will not waste the opportunity to let you know in this moment.

Remember, one of the signs that your wife is healing is that the feeling of bringing you in on her deepest feelings goes from fear to comfort. For her to go from fear to comfort in that regard, you must also go from egotistical to humble, kind, and considerate. The hindrances to that will likely be in an attachment to tradition, preoccupation with how it makes you look to outsiders, and/or a lack of a developing relationship with God.

Discuss this with your wife and ask if she'll be open to guiding you as to which of those she believes you struggle with. As she brings you in on her healing fight, get in the habit of also bringing her in on your journey of becoming an ally. You won't always get this right, but the process of putting your best foot forward together, with her, will add to the re-connectedness you're pursuing.

Note to the healing spouse:

Get crystal clear about how you feel ego has presented itself in the relationship thus far. What specific scenarios has it shown up? How could things have gone differently for you to have drawn closer to your husband instead? The more clearly you can define these issues, the better you can ensure he has the keys to fully turn things around in this area.

Keep in mind, a toxic ego is so normalized in our society that many men see it as just a part of who they are. If you're thinking that "normal" doesn't make it right, you're correct. But taking time to articulate exactly how it has resulted in you pushing away from your husband will effectively communicate why it's not right and give him the opportunity to act on that information to achieve his own goal of being close to you again.

Remember, one of the signs you're healing is when you're able to be vulnerable again as opposed to going into your shell like you'd normally do. Him checking his own ego, specific to you, is going to pave the way for that vulnerability. But first, you must be specific about exactly what that looks like.

Chapter 8

The Trail of Tears

A broken heart is a master manipulator.

It will tell you life is not worth living. It will tell you that no one can ever love you, or that your relationship can never be restored, all of which are the biggest lies the heartbroken tend to fall victim to.

Because those lies are so convincing at the height of our pain, I've seen people who act from that vantage point causing damage that can be difficult to live down. From homicide to revenge cheating, a broken heart can have you unrecognizable to yourself based on the decisions you make.

Healing spouses who still want to heal both individually and with their spouse experience this the most. While others who decided to just leave their relationship can simply block that part of their life out or settle on their ex deserving every bit of it, the healing partner who chooses to stay is also choosing to face and reckon with the aftermath of their reaction to being hurt.

Take Clarissa for example. She was known as an incredibly sweet, loving, and kind woman to all who knew her. She was a stay-at-home mom looking to finish her Ph.D. in theology that she'd begun before having two children with her husband Ryan.

Unfortunately, Ryan had cheated with multiple women and his wife found out via texts messages in his phone one late night while he was in the shower. Clarissa said nothing, completely shocked, but when Ryan went to work the next day, she called her mother to come and help her pack her things and their two toddlers, and they left the house.

While Ryan was not honoring his marital vows, he absolutely adored his two children and was very involved in their lives since the day they were born. So, needless to say, when he got the call from their preschool that they'd not shown up to school that day, he was worried. That worry increased tenfold when he couldn't get through to Clarissa's phone since she'd blocked all calls and texts as she and her mother were already driving the children 1,500 miles away from their home. She would only respond to him via email a few days later to tell him they were safe, but nothing more.

Over the following eight months of what became their separation, she continued to occasionally block Ryan from communicating with or seeing their children, knowing how bad it hurt him. She drug his name through the mud to those who would listen, verbally abused him with hurtful information only she knew about his childhood, and conspired with her male friends to make it look like she was sexually involved with them so Ryan would get that impression and maybe feel some level of the pain she did.

Admittedly, she wasn't her best self in this time, but she couldn't feel an ounce of sympathy or remorse. Compared to the way she felt, she figured it was a slap on the wrist, and she wanted him to get as many slaps as it would take to ensure he would learn his lesson.

You may wonder, *"Why didn't she just leave the jerk instead?"*

Well, after taking the children and going away from Ryan, Clarissa quickly learned of a few more details that made her think twice about writing him off. Ryan had proof that he had already ended the affairs months prior to her learning of them as well as the professional help he'd hired to guide him on the best way to confess without allowing things to spill over into their children's lives. Keeping it from her for any amount of time was a risk he knew he was taking, but due to how his parents' rocky marriage affected him and his siblings in their adult lives, he didn't want to pass the same trauma to his children. This didn't justify the affairs nor keeping them hidden from Clarissa, but the context was less malicious than she originally thought.

Also, shortly before his first infidelity, he'd developed a heavy alcohol addiction but was able to hide it from his wife by coming home after she was already sleep so that by the time she woke, the stench was no longer on him. With receipts to prove he was spending $300-400 a week on alcohol and his thirty-day AA program he'd completed to end the addiction, Ryan came clean about every aspect of this dark period in his life where he spiraled out of control, but also the tangible measures he'd taken to course-correct. His shame motivated his secrecy, not his desire to continue on in his ways.

He was well aware that none of this was an excuse for stepping out on his wife, and before being found out about any of it, had already dedicated his life to Christ, gotten professional help, and ended all of these destructive behaviors so that he could return to being the husband

Clarissa deserved, all of which, there was verifiable evidence for at least. He profusely expressed deep remorse and was willing to do whatever it would take to restore the marriage back to full strength, so Clarissa saw this as a reason to give it a try even though she'd already left the marriage home.

However, her heart couldn't unshatter so easily, and as she commenced her own dark period of spiraling, she did everything she could to break him before returning to him.

Ryan's new relationship with Christ is what he credits to being able to weather the storm, but that didn't stop him from getting struck by Clarissa's lightning. Once Clarissa began returning to her healed self and knowing that her marriage was an emotionally safe place for her, she suffered tremendous guilt of the marriage's new wounds from her return-fire during their separation.

The children were now triggered when seeing their father leave the house because during the separation, they never knew when Clarissa would allow them to see him again. Ryan was receiving disingenuous reviews on his business from friends of friends who she'd brought into their marital issues, as they sought revenge on her behalf. This caused a major drop in his and his family's income, which caused their marriage home to go into foreclosure. Clarissa's mother refused to allow him at her house with the rest of his family, so he was forced to go to an extended-stay hotel while trying to resurrect his company's reputation.

I sat and listened one day as Clarissa detailed all of this over the phone. She'd joined my Self-Crowned VIP mentorship group in the worst part of her separation, looking to draw motivation to continue torturing Ryan as retribution for the pain she'd felt, but instead she found herself convicted as she slowly realized she was becoming the version of him who hurt her.

She had no interest in acting like Ryan was a victim, since he caused the situation to begin with, but she couldn't deny that the aftermath was partly her fault. He hadn't blamed her for her response to his affairs, but her reactions were taking a life of their own, a life that was bringing death to the marriage they were hoping to rebuild.

This is more or less extreme than the situation you may find yourself in, but I'll tell you like I told her, "It's going to be okay, but only if you commit two things. First, stop the bleeding. Second, stitch the wounds."

What's done is already done, but it needs to stop, as well as "stitches" need to be put in place.

For Clarissa, this meant making the outsiders go back outside again. Her mother, friends, and their church family she'd given front row seats to their saga had to get curtains closed on them.

This was easier said than done because these weren't people who meant her harm. In fact, they only got invested to help bear Clarissa's burden of heartbreak with her. What if they felt used from being told to now mind their business, when she was the one calling their phones begging for someone to listen? What if she needed them again later, and this time they turned their backs on her? Things still weren't perfect between her and Ryan, and she didn't want to risk isolating herself from the support system she leaned on to survive. She toggled between the guilt of allowing this problem to persist and the reluctance to do anything about it.

I asked, "Do you believe these people you've brought into your marriage issues truly love you?" She answered, "Yes, well, some of them. My mother and my friends, for sure."

"Okay," I responded. "Trust in that love to also love the process of being there for you when you need someone, and also stepping back when you need that as well. Trust that your best interest is what they have at heart, not their desire to be directly involved. Also, ask them to trust you and your judgment of the current situation and what is required to continue moving forward."

She looked as if she hadn't thought of that before. She wasn't completely relieved, but rather fearful, in a good way. She had the kind of fear we all have when we're stepping out of what has become our comfort zone, in which her marital separation lynch mob members had become hers.

It was time for her to hit the reset button on the support system she had militarized so they could either come back into support of her and her current needs or expose their true selfish motives.

The reset button looked like this:

- Discussing, with her husband Ryan the new Relationship Membrane (reference my book: *Don't Forget Your Crown: Self-love Has Everything to Do With It*). Coming to an agreement with him to clarify what boundaries he'd like on those outside the marriage allowed the teamwork dynamic to be re-established within and prevent future conflict.

- Addressing her friends and family she had any continued dialogue with and thanking them for being a soft place to land during her turmoil.

- Affirming the value they brought to her while also stating how different her perspective is now that she's in a much better place, but still healing, daily.

- Asking for their help in a different way, going forward, and explaining that this way would be in letting her figure things out strictly between God and her husband. In this she affirmed that it wasn't a reflection of a change on their friendship, just a part of the shift for what she's trying to accomplish.

- Before ending the conversation, she also made sure to restore honor to Ryan by affirming that he'd taken the steps she felt comfortable with to trust in the chance she was giving him again. She resisted going too far into detail, as she wasn't looking for their approval, but out of consideration for their concern, was allowing them the opportunity to also feel at ease.

From there, she gave the rest to God to reveal, which, if any of her friends and family loved her more than they had learned to hate her husband, this would be a test for them as much as a revelation for her going forward.

However, this was only the beginning. She also had to hit the reset button on the damaged relationship between him and their children. The youngest son had picked up on her resentment for him and had become increasingly rebellious to

Ryan. No matter how much Ryan tried to love on the child or lovingly discipline him, the two-year-old now had the same aversion to being receptive that he witnessed from his mother.

Unfortunately, children aren't always able to put into context the relationship of their parents and separate that from how they should operate. This is why it's best for parents to make the separation on a daily basis in how they treat each other while the children are around.

The Bible says that we are to train a child up the way in which they should go, and when they grow up, they will not depart from it (Proverbs 22:6 KJV). Real life has taught any parent that children will do what they see you do before they do what you tell them to. Therefore, to restore the relationship her children had with Ryan, Clarissa had to retrain her children by showing them displays of affection and respect towards him. She would even defer questions they'd ask to her to him so that they reassociated his position in the home with authority.

Since Ryan was equally committed to making sure he didn't abuse his position as leader of the house, Clarissa didn't have to prioritize a defense against that, but rather could focus on teaching the children that their father was safe to love, listen to, and model after.

In just one month, the fear and confusion Clarissa once had was replaced with peace of mind since her external environment of safety was now consistent with her marital and internal environment. Her guilt had waned and she found joy in seeing the children now able to receive their father's love. But, she realized a new problem.

Ryan was suffering also. Clarissa didn't feel a moral obligation to tend to that as much as she missed the masculine edge he had before she began verbally abusing him into passivity. The confidence he had before the separation that was attractive to her as well as vanished after months of throwing his wrongdoings in his face to remind him how much he failed his family. In addition to seemingly futile efforts to restore his business, he was afraid to fully apply himself, for fear that he might cause her to regress back to a lack of safety with his priorities.

Clarissa didn't want that. She wanted the man she fell in love with, which included his ambition. She just wanted the upgraded version of him with his new commitment to Christ and perspective on how to properly protect her heart.

Ironically, there was now a need to restore Ryan in a similar fashion to the way he was being an ally to help restore her and their marriage.

I knew she'd face this challenge, but allowed her to first realize it before showing her the way to execute a plan to get her husband back. This is one of the toughest realizations to come to as a healing spouse, and also one of the last things we tend to grasp on to for confidence things will be different.

But don't get it confused. There's a difference between a wounded spouse and a changed spouse. Seeing them aching from the way their consequences have affected them isn't evidence that they have a new heart, and a new heart doesn't require a betraying spouse to indefinitely ache.

For complete restoration and healing of a marriage, starting with the healing spouse, there must be a restoration of the ally as well.

Why? Because we make our worst decisions when we're feeling our worst. Our danger zone is when we feel broken, discouraged, angry, depleted, overwhelmed, or insufficient. That's when we drop our standards and fall for illusions of comfort.

While the pain of our bad decisions is helpful to serve as a reminder, a perpetual state of being stuck in that low state will not only diminish any attractiveness our spouse once had, it reproduces the same result as the first bad decision, just using a different method to do so.

The things Clarissa needed from Ryan, beyond just the restoration of her safety, but to effectively love all around, could only be provided by the best version of Ryan. Clarissa, being the closest to him and the most meaningful person in his life had the keys to create that more than anyone else, so long as she could finally forsake the safety she'd identified in his broken state.

Once I had confirmation from her that she was ready to wipe her hands with that old perspective, and completely commit to showing the ultimate grace of a healing spouse with her redemptive love, it was easy to help her achieve her goal of experiencing that attractiveness with Ryan again, like before.

Ryan's love language was Words of Affirmation, so Clarissa made a daily commitment to speak life into every positive thing he did. For the things he didn't do so well, she mentioned them only after reaffirming how much she appreciated him and just before reassuring him of her confidence in him as a man.

If he helped with the dishes, she told him she appreciated it. If he brought groceries into the home, she thanked him and hugged him a little tighter. If he left the toilet seat up, she first thanked him for something completely unrelated, then asked him if he'd be more mindful of the toilet seat in the future, then proceeded with reassuring him that she appreciated his commitment to put it down next time.

These things may seem menial, but every day that Clarissa filled the air with her words of affirmation toward Ryan, especially in areas she'd used her tongue to slice him to shreds, she saw healing before her eyes.

Ryan had checked his ego long ago, so her words empowered his ability to be the compassionate leader she needed. He felt more and more comfortable operating in his professional element since his wife was making it clear she was there to have his back, not hold him back. He enthusiastically looked for new ways to serve Clarissa, motivated by opportunities to earn more expressed appreciation from her. The docility in his demeanor vanished, allowing him to exude the masculine, assertive, protective energy that Clarissa and the children gravitated to more than ever before.

This is consistent with the dating principle that "Broken people break people." The energy we give out typically comes from the reserve we have stored within. If a person is broken and in no way interested in healing, it will come second nature to break everyone else who gets close. That's why in the dating phase, it's imperative that we both avoid dealing with and being that person.

However, the same concept applies vice versa. So, in Clarissa's progress in her healing, she had developed the capacity to transmit that healing onto Ryan without losing momentum in hers. She didn't have to be complete in hers to give Ryan the support he needed in his, and once she realized that, she additionally created the environment she longed for in their marriage.

Chapter 9

Re-Sexducation 101

"I made a covenant with mine eyes; why then should I think upon a maid?" Job 31:1 KJV

A lot has been said about the amount of patience and restraint required to be in close proximity to a healing woman. Nonetheless, let's not kid ourselves. No matter how spiritual, remorseful, or committed you are to being a resource for your wife's healing, you're still a human, and humans desire sex.

The Bible vouches for this in 1 Corinthians 7:3-5, stating how spouses are to fulfill each other's sexual needs and how our bodies don't not exclusively belong to us, but rather to our spouses. Unfortunately, this scripture has also been leveraged by many to justify pressuring wives into meeting a husband's sexual needs at the expense of the wives' unmet emotional needs. Even worse, I've lost count of the number of men I've personally witnessed fall victim to the naivety that when a wife resists this pressure, it is "punishment."

My mouth hit the floor during a heated discussion between a woman at our table and a gentleman who'd stood on this belief to the point of nearly shedding tears. We were supposed to be enjoying a nice dinner and celebrating our pastor's 20th anniversary in ministry, but instead, my wife and I got an earful about how immoral a wife is if she doesn't want to have sex, and even how a husband has the right to step out if she doesn't give him sex.

From the tone of his voice, I knew it was mostly frustration that motivated the man's sentiments, not Biblical principle or anything remotely close to logic.

The Bible repeatedly condemns infidelity, stresses how a husband's love is to be sacrificial, and that we are to be kind to our wives. There's nothing kind about telling a wife she must have sex despite feeling repulsed by the thought. In 1 Corinthians 7:6, Paul also goes on to state that the charge to meet our spouse's sexual needs is not a commandment, meaning it's not a mandate, ever. However, it is suggested, but there's a much more effective way to go about that, especially when loving a woman who's healing.

Again, sexual desire is not evil, but sex is also not an entitlement by mere virtue of being married. As an ally, it's understandable that you want to have sex, but you must first understand the rules of a woman's brakes and accelerators.

The best breakdown of this I've seen is described as *The Dual Model* by Dr. Emily Nagoski, expert on women's sexual health and author of the *New York Times* best seller, *Come As You Are*. *The Dual Model* explains the ways the brain responds to stimuli that either decrease arousal in the form of "brakes" or increase arousal in the form of "accelerators." Brakes are things the brain registers as a threat, whether it be the feeling of being used, potential STD, fear of impact to reputation, etc. Conversely, accelerators are things or feelings that increase a woman's desire for sex like pleasant smell, attractiveness, comfort, etc.

While every woman is different, studies show that over 70% of women are much more sensitive to their brakes than accelerators, whereas the exact opposite is true for men. When both accelerators and brakes are present at the same time, men tend to be more highly influenced by our accelerators. Meanwhile in the same situation, a woman can be completely shut down by the smallest brake. Furthermore, when women are in a highly stressed emotional state, i.e., healing from heartbreak, her sensitivity to her brakes goes up and so do the number of things that her mind will register as such.

What does this mean? This means that if a man only understands decisions to sexually engage through his own firsthand lens, he's going to be miles away from how a woman makes the same decision, even in intramarital healing. This will leave him lost in a situation where his wife is not sexually engaging with him for any reason.

Every man will eventually experience frustrations and occasional feelings of disconnectedness with his wife. However, his sexual desire for her won't be affected so long as the accelerators are there. If she maintains a relatively similar physical shape that attracted him, or her eyes are still the pretty color they were when he became mesmerized with them, the brakes of the marital turmoil are almost powerless to stop him from wanting sex.

Because of that, men tend to check one box when searching for reasons their wives aren't sexually engaging: Are things that used to turn her on still present? If that answer is yes, then the only reason a wife wouldn't satisfy her husband's need is because she's making a conscious decision to make him pay. Yet studies show that some wives not only desire to meet their husband's needs, but experience fleeting sensations of sexual arousal, yet struggle to translate any of that into sexual action. She even may have no clue as to why herself.

During the healing process, she may be sexually attracted to your nice abs, fresh haircut, or new suit, but her brakes are suppressing her arousal like a chokehold from *The Incredible Hulk*. If the sparks of sexual arousal do come, they won't be enough to catch a flame despite a desperate desire to do so. Orgasming may be difficult, if it happens at all, and a feeling of regret will follow the sex, preventing it in the future.

The mistake men often make in this situation is trying to ramp up the accelerators: new cologne, more foreplay, going on a romantic getaway, gifts, spending more time in the gym, etc. Why? Because we figure she's likely just unimpressed by the old accelerators, and now it's time to step our game up. After all, that's what dwindles our sexual desire. If you've ever heard of a man's complaints about his sex life, particularly when it comes to his inability to be aroused by his wife, it's almost always something to do with the wife's underwear choices, workout regiment, diet, hair choice, or some other physical aesthetic.

So, to reignite our wife's sexual desire, we do our best to level up our accelerators, but when our wife doesn't respond favorably, we take it personally, but we shouldn't. The truth is women are wired differently from men, so increasing her sexual desire to match ours won't be a matter of increasing her accelerators but removing the brakes instead.

Let me repeat: **More sex from your wife means less brakes, not more accelerators.**

So, for a woman who is healing, what does this mean?

Let's just take a worst-case scenario and say some type of sexual immorality has caused the wedge currently between you and your wife. Whether you had sex with another woman outside the relationship, got that woman pregnant, contracted an STD, developed an addiction to porn, or had a long-time habit of blurring the lustful line with women on social media, the effect almost definitely has not pushed her to fulfill your need more. In this case, betrayal isn't just a "brake," it has practically run her desire for sex into a brick wall.

Women who tolerated a sexually immoral husband commonly describe their emotional state during sex in very similar ways. Perpetual feelings of disgust, distrust, anger, self-pity, fear, personally feeling like a prostitute, and wanting to throw up are just a few descriptors women have used by these women causing sex to eventually come to a halt.

So, what can you do in this position of sexually disgusting your wife while still desiring sex? Firstly, un-disgust yourself by putting a hard stop to things that caused your disconnect with her, many of which are likely brakes to her desire.

Based on Biblical principle, psychology, and my personal experience, I've compiled a quick list of twenty things every man can use to get started.

Things That Will Make Her Sexually Withdraw From You

1. Staring at another woman's body.
2. Looking directly at a woman's buttocks or breasts more than once after accidentally doing so the first time.
3. Watching pornography.
4. Watching videos of women wearing "yoga pants" or skin-tight gym wear.
5. Letting women chat it up with you without acknowledging your wife.
6. Looking back at women who walk by.
7. Watching movies with explicit sex scenes.
8. Looking at lingerie pictures in magazines or online.
9. Following accounts online showcasing women's bodies.
10. Following women online you don't know due to their attractiveness.
11. Following women online you do know due to their attractiveness.
12. Following women online you've had a sexual encounter with, ever.
13. Expressing physical compliments or acknowledgement of women online or in real life.
14. Having coffee or lunch outings with women present that your wife isn't made aware of or in approval of beforehand.
15. Responding favorably in any way to women who flirt with you.
16. Listening to music that sexually objectifies women in general.
17. Masturbating.
18. Comparing her to previous sexual encounters with other women.

19. Participating in sexual conversations with other women (unless for professional purposes, i.e., HIV awareness and prevention).
20. Allowing women to call or text you that your wife doesn't know.

"Now, that's just unrealistic."
"If she needs all that, she's just too insecure."

If you thought something like this, then you're just like me when I focused too much on the rules and not enough on the reward.

You don't have to be a Bible scholar to know something about the Adam and Eve story. I'll give you a quick summary: God told them they could eat of any tree in the Garden of Eden except one, and they ate from that one.

The number of rules wasn't the problem then, and it isn't now. The problem was that Adam and Eve never considered the potential reward of following the rule; first and foremost, a guaranteed trip to heaven when they died. But also, the gratification of the other trees in the garden. Instead, they were deceived into only focusing on what they would miss out on by avoiding the forbidden fruit.

Let's look at the list of things not to do in order to keep from pushing your wife away as the "Forbidden Fruit" list. While the instant gratification of those things you may be giving up are present are your mind, have you thought about the long-term satisfaction that could take its place if you follow the rules to stay away from those things?

What if you had a wife who had no second thoughts about your compliments to her because they're not overshadowed with recent memories of you gawking at other women on social media? What if your wife never had to question your respect for her feelings because the evidence of it was obvious in the way you set boundaries with other women?

Your wife would have less brakes, which means much more acceleration towards meeting your sexual needs, even as she's healing. Sex wouldn't be followed by her regret, so you'd get more and more as time went on, without even asking. The sex would bring you two closer instead of pushing her as far from you as possible and finding new ways to avoid your requests for sex. The intimacy would not only be pleasurable, but medicinal to the marriage in general, furthering the cause of restoring the wife back to full emotional strength.

This would be the equivalent to the sweet taste of the other trees Adam and Eve were allowed to eat from, in which if they'd focused on that, would likely have had no problem staying away from the one tree that came at the price of their relationship with God. In the case of being an ally to your wife, the forbidden fruit could cost your marriage.

So, what's your next step?

It's time to Re-sexducate yourself. Forget everything you've been told by previous sexual partners. Ignore the things you learned from pornography. Scrap what your uncles and older male cousins told you when you were an adolescent. It's time to relearn sex, especially as it relates to meeting your wife's sexual needs. You may even need to help her learn what her needs are for her herself.

First, see what idea she has of her needs, but refrain from startling her. The more defensive she is during your questioning, the less you will get the answers you're looking for.

Start with something like, "Hey, I got a question. I'm not looking to have sex or ask you for it, but it is a sexual question. Is it okay that I ask?" The effort to handle this topic with care could remove a brake before she even speaks.

Once she gives you the green light to go forward with your question, allow her to take the lead on whatever you're asking. Here are a few examples that can get you started.

1. "What was the best sexual experience for you strictly as it pertains to your own experience? What do you remember being special about it?"
2. "Do you ever catch yourself having thoughts while having sex that take you out of the moment? What are they?"
3. "How long does it normally take you from the time that I first touch you until we're actually having sex for you to feel completely comfortable?"
4. "Is there anything new about the way I touch your body that I need to know before we have sex again?"
5. "In the past, have I done anything that made you uncomfortable in the bedroom?"
6. "On a scale of 1 to 10, how comfortable are you with telling me when you don't want to have sex? What can I do to increase that comfort?"

7. "Would you be willing to be completely selfish next time and solely help me learn how to create the absolute best experience for you?"

Of course, these are just a few. You may even look at these and feel like you already know the answer, but still, run them by your wife and have her verify whether or not you're correct. Again, and I can't stress this enough, make sure you wait until it's the right time. If you're getting clear indicators, and you ask the preliminary question first, there should be no doubt on when exactly that will be.

What you're doing in this process is completing your dating-phase detox. You're unlearning the problematic patterns most of us picked up before we knew the consequences of indulging in sexcapades with people before we were married. Too many people feel judged at the thought of being mindful of these drawbacks, so they ignore the reality that if you have premarital sex with every person you "think" could be the one for you, you're setting yourself up for sexual satisfactory failure with your actual spouse in the future.

I've previously discussed that contrary to popular belief, being single is not for doing what you want, but rather for preparing for what you want. If you want to ace an exam, you don't prepare by staying up all night and partying the night before. You prepare by studying, getting some rest, and coming to the test clear-headed.

The same thing goes for marital sex. We can't expect to get anything higher than a D if before the marital sex test, we stayed out all night partying and drinking. And we're sure to get an F if we don't study, but rather think we'll figure everything out once it's time to start marking our answers. If you've been failing due to your behavior prior to marriage, the key to passing with flying colors will require you to study and clear your mind.

Clearing your mind is the detox. Studying is the re-sexducation, and once you do this, your previous sexual experience will pale in comparison to your sex life going forward.

Chapter 10

Why Guarded Women Are a Blessing

"Her children arise up, and call her blessed; her husband also, and he praiseth her." Proverbs 31:28 KJV

A wise man once said, "We should expect two marriages in our lifetime, sometimes to the same person." He wasn't referring to being married, divorcing, and then later on reconnecting with the same person, although sometimes that does happen. What he was referring to was the reality that most people who get married don't have the slightest clue of what it really means to be married and end up learning that through some extremely difficult circumstances that require them to rebuild their marriage from the ground up in order to survive.

Once your wife is on the other side of her healing, you will find this to be your reality as well. She has now been shaped by painful experiences, although no longer dominated by them. She has learned new things about herself and life in general that will shape the way she deals with you and pursues her personal goals. This is the healed version of your wife, upgraded and evolved.

Therefore, you will need to get with the same program in order to remain compatible.

As you begin noticing signs of your wife being restored, don't think in the context of the woman you once knew. Yes, she will still be in the same body and have many of the same personality traits. However, her convictions have been refined and her trust in those convictions are greater than ever. If you present old ways that alert her intuition that something still isn't right, she will not betray her best judgment again.

So, as you get to know the new her, continue the pursuit of making the old version of you that had any part of her previous wounds a distant memory. Shed your old dead skin. Any laziness, lack of priorities, dismissiveness, inconsistencies, etc. on a personal level should receive your corrective attention as her healing is nearing its end.

In real life, what does that look like?

Firstly, start the dating process all over again. Introduce questions, conversations, and activities that allow you to gather data on whom you're now dealing with. Don't do so in a way that's sarcastic as it will show an insensitivity to the process she's freshly coming out of. Rather, deal with her with a heightened level of optimistic intrigue about the new woman your privileged to be able to love.

Start in the places you would normally assume that you know her. For instance, if you're about to turn on the TV after both of you are sitting on the couch, don't immediately turn on any particular program. Ask her, "What kind of things are you into watching these days? I know you used to love home renovation shows, but has anything else caught your attention lately?"

Something so simple as that will begin to create a welcoming environment to all of the ways she may have changed. Instead of contributing to an environment of pressure on her to make sure that she doesn't make you uncomfortable by the new things she's intrigued by, this will allow her comfort to bring you into this new phase of her life that she is embracing. By embracing it with you, you allow yourself to be a part of what is now a shared journey, which is another way of ensuring that the two of you are growing together, not apart.

Another question you could ask while out is something like, "I stopped by the mall to pick up some new underwear. Which ones are your favorite color on me?" The first thought through her mind is that you would already know what her favorite color is on you, but if you have zero sarcasm in your tone, she will be charmed that you were open to her suggestion and your awareness that this is a completely new her. Not only that, you are reiterating your high level of regard for what she finds attractive instead of implicating that what she sees is what she's going to get. Without verbalizing it, you reaffirmed the importance of her feelings while flirting with her, all at the same time. Once you've been the ally your wife needs in her healing, you now must communicate that you fully support the healed version of her in the ways you integrate yourself into her renewed life.

As for making the version of you that contributed to the broken version of her in the past a distant memory, that will require a few more measures, most of which you should have begun developing when you shifted from being her spouse to her ally in her healing journey.

So, you've already ended any betrayals or related behavior. You've also come completely clean to her and disowned your ego. You even went so far as taking all the steps necessary to de-disgust yourself as it pertains to her sexual attraction to you.

That, and the various other actionable steps will be evidence of your evolution, but for those allies who also prefer to overachieve, here's a cheat sheet for going that extra mile:

1. Compliment her with detail.

For example, instead of complimenting her by saying, "You look nice today." You can say, "Wow, I'm loving that new blouse. The color really brings out the brown in your eyes. Is that the one you got from House of CB last month?" Of course, you don't have to say that exactly. This example simply shows more effort and indicates that on a regular basis you pay close attention to her and what she's into. Instead of complimenting her in a lazy fashion that may imply you just want to get it over with, the attention to detail and question on the end signals effort. Yes, this will feel weird to you if you didn't talk like this before, but as we discussed in the previous chapter, give yourself a chance to taste the rewards before you knock it.

2. Listen to understand.

We covered this earlier, but it's worth the re-emphasis. For example, during a verbal conflict, stay away from phrases like, "So, you mean to tell me…," followed by some distorted version of what she actually said that requires her to defend herself and only representative of your feelings about what she said. Instead, with a gentle and compassionate tone, say something like, "Okay, thank you for the explaining that but I want to make sure that I'm understanding you correctly so please let me know if I am. What you just said is..." and finish this sentence reiterating not only what you genuinely believe she said, but what your perception is of the meaning behind what she just said.

Again, make sure that this is laced in love and compassion, not in some effort to win a debate. Remember, your ego is dead, don't let any hurt feelings revive it. For every time you listen to understand, you reiterate the growth from who you once were, which breathes life into her growing confidence that she made the right decision by working this marriage out with you.

3. Allow her to make mistakes.

If your wife has been diligent in her therapy and healing process, there are sure to be rules around what she should not do that would only cause her to regress. Chances are, as her ally, you've been made aware of at least some of these. However, even though she may be a healed version of herself now, she will still be an imperfect version of herself who is trying her best to settle into this new life. Even in cases that her actions offend, hurt, or even trigger you because they remind you of the version of her that wasn't healed, don't forget that you are her still her ally first and foremost. Not her lecturer, teacher, disciplinarian, and definitely not her enemy. So, when she makes the wrong move, and she will, constantly reaffirm her efforts to stay away from those types of mistakes as well as the progress in her you're still grateful for. To avoid doing this in a way that comes off condescending, try something like this, "It's okay that you missed our lunch date. I know things happen, and one mistake doesn't change the fact that I know you take our time together seriously. You have proven that too many times for me to doubt that now. I love you and I needed to fast anyway. Lol." A sense of humor may not be your forte, but if you have one, use it after genuinely communicating your compassionate stance with her. Your grace will go a long way.

4. Grab your pom-poms.

Believe it or not, marketing is not just for business owners. In everything that we do, we are associating a meaning to the outside world about who we are and what we represent, and hopefully we're doing so in the way that's valuable to us. This is marketing in a nutshell, and while we never want to focus on the outside opinions, it always helps to make clear to the outside world that you're each other's biggest fans. It's similar to the saying, "You teach people how to respect you by how you respect yourself." Well, in a relationship, you teach outsiders to respect you and your wife as a team by constantly representing that, including when it comes to support and edification of each other.

In exalting your wife publicly, you are letting everyone know that you know what kind of blessing you have at home. You have her back. You're not just happy with your choice, but you're grateful that choice also chose you. It's a public declaration that you honor her, and therefore sets the tone for those who come into your circle to do the same.

Moreover, it increases the barrier between you and other women's hope of having a chance with you. Let me make this clear, this does not mean telling all of your intimate business and secrets to the public. This is making an acknowledgement that clarifies any confusion on your wife's part or the general public's part about how proud you are of your wife and grateful you are to have her in your life.

If you do this without begging for attention or some type of reward in return, your wife will appreciate it. As a woman, she understands the message it sends to other women, and it's exactly the message that needs to be sent. The message is that other women can't compete because there is no competition. Your wife has won, and you've won because you have her.

5. Invite accountability.
I know it seems that by executing the concepts in his book, the expectation is that you're pretty much perfect, but that's not the case. You don't have to be perfect to be real.

A part of being real, is being real with someone else who can hold you accountable. The first one you should be accountable to is God, and secondly, your wife. Invite her accountability by saying things like, "Hey, I know you told me to let you know if I may be working with any female clients, and I had one book an appointment for tomorrow at 3 p.m. Just wanted to check and see if it was okay to confirm. If not, I can refer her to another consultant or make our meeting virtual instead, no problem."

This approach communicates the utmost regard for your wife, while making sure you're meeting her standards for what's appropriate instead of just yours. You also take any responsibility off of her to consider appropriate alternatives that will align with previously expressed boundaries, so that you don't come off intentionally obtuse or independent.

Go even further by creating a schedule that she has access to. This isn't just about recovery or healing, this is model behavior for healthy couples, period. While both you should be allowed to have your own individual lives, there's never a place you should be that your wife shouldn't be able to know about. This goes back to the breeding grounds for betrayal and only ego or illicit behavior would prevent you from allowing her into your daily whereabouts and activities.

As you can see, creating a healing environment within your marriage is not just about what you do while your spouse is healing, but how you prevent additional events that will cause the need for healing in the future. That starts with understanding that marriages are never stagnant. They're either going up or going down, all dependent on the two people controlling the steering wheel.

So, never get it in your head that you've arrived. Even I have been guilty of this. The smallest positive changes result in massive shifts in the marriage and satisfaction sets in, but don't let it. Get some accountability partners, personal mentors, marital mentors, Godly resources, prayer, as well as your wife's regular input on how well you're meeting her needs to keep you constantly pushing forward.

You and your wife will enjoy the fruits of both of your labors, but so will your children, if you have them or plan on having them. Your career will flourish, now that your mind isn't showing up to work drained from the environment at home. Your health will improve from the decrease in stress that marital turmoil brings. Your emotional needs will be met now that you have a wife who doesn't wake up every day scratching for survival. These are just a few benefits of contributing to not only your wife's healing, but in having a properly loved woman in your corner altogether.

As men of God, we should also consider that our wives don't actually belong to us but rather to God. If we claim to love Him, we need to show it in part by how we love the blessing He put in our lives--His daughter. A part of love is how you redeem someone from their lowest point through grace, patience, and long-suffering. Love doesn't leave you at your lowest, and it also doesn't keep you at your lowest. It redeems you back to your full strength and continues to make you stronger.

In a relationship context, love alone is never enough, but it's a start. The rest of what your wife needs comes from your commitment to her, God, and foremost to yourself. Don't be fooled into thinking things would be better if you just moved on to someone else who doesn't need to heal from anything either. Could it be easier? Sure.

However, it would only be easier if you encountered a woman who's 100% healed from all past betrayals, which is unlikely since those women typically achieve that with the help of a man who didn't run from that healing process and are currently with them. Most single women who've ever been in a serious relationship are still in the process of healing in some aspect, which would still require the same contribution from you to create a healing environment in the relationship.

To avoid all women who have anything to heal from would be to only date those who have never gone through anything that requires them to heal. Again, those women may be "easier" to be with, but not necessarily better.

Women who've overcome pain and adversity in any aspect of their lives have developed a level of strength uncommon to those who've never been hurt at all. Same thing goes for men. If you audit your own strength and tenacity, you'll likely link the development of those traits back to something difficult that pushed you to attain these qualities to survive.

This isn't to shame women who've never encountered the darkest sides of life and relationships, but rather to put in perspective that they're typically not battle tested like the women who've made it through some storms. Women who've been humiliated at some point have a much stronger conviction about bringing honor to their husbands who honor them. Women who've been heartbroken before tend to be uncompromising in protecting the heart of the one they love whom also protects their heart. Women who've had their minds toyed with value transparency and straightforwardness more than those women who don't know the torture of such an experience. Women who've been left high and dry will stick with the ones they love through the absolute worst in life because they know what it feels like to be left stranded.

Unfortunately, these women have also been preyed on because of what they've been through, so they also can be understandably guarded, but that's the point of being your wife's ally. She knows what kind of man you can be. She knows what you have been at your best. She needs to see proof that the worst of you is no longer allowed to hurt her. Once you prove that to her, which won't be easy, you'll find it more than worth it due to the way she's grown from those hurtful experiences. Yes, her standards for you will be higher and any tolerance for future "mistakes" will be less, but she will come out of this hurt a much better version of herself. As a better version of yourself, you'll be able to fully appreciate that unlike before.

You won't have to guess about whether or not she's going to be there for you should you get sick and lose your job. You're the man who defeated his lowest self to love her back to full strength and never hurt her again. She's going to be right there with you. You won't have to fear being left for another man who's taller or makes more money. When her world was shaken up, it was the character of whom you are that she found safety in, not vain things, so those vain things won't impress her. She'll be locked in with the one who locked in with her when most would run.

A woman who's never been through anything won't have the pedigree to automatically respond the same way to those types of life events. In fact, she could make it worse. She would have no respect for facing difficulty in life and therefore ridicule you for your difficulty to, which you will have. Your discouragement or frustration in life won't be something she can truly relate to, and therefore could be misinterpreted as weakness to attack you for instead of an opportunity to build you up.

Essentially, don't think the grass is greener on the other side. It may look that way because it's fake, a façade, and an illusion of things being better if you took the "easy" route cowards take when faced with the task to help their wives heal. Your own grass can and will continue to be restored if you roll up your sleeves and get to work, and no feeling will compare to knowing you did once you're done.

Chapter 11:

When It "Doesn't Work"

I received this email about four months before the publishing of this book, and immediately halted the release so that I could include it. It read:

"He left. Thanks for nothing."

I was told by my agent to leave this part out, but I have no interest in hiding the truth from you. The cold, hard reality is that sometimes, there's nothing left to do but let go.

Carol came to that conclusion after she and her husband Neal began the intramarital healing process.

She'd asked for my help in recovering all that'd been lost due to Neal's online emotional affair. Initially, he was all ears for what he needed to do to restore Carol's trust and hold on to their six-year marriage. She had decided she could get past his double life so long as he ended it and renewed the vows of the marriage to make it new.

Only a month into the process, Neal decided that he would rather just pursue a relationship with his online affair partner in England whom he'd never met and leave Carol with their three-year-old daughter in Wisconsin where they'd built a life together.

Upon coming home from work and seeing his clothes drawers emptied and a note on their kitchen counter telling her he was, "sorry," she sent me that email.

I wasn't surprised.

I'd been keeping up with her via my weekly live chats to my Self-Crowned VIP community, and Carol was doing the work. She noticed when her amygdala was being hijacked. She averted opportunities for revenge and removed herself instead. She followed the steps to create internal safety, clearly expressed boundaries needed for her trust to be rebuilt, and even began re-sexducating him on her sexual brakes and accelerators so they could revive their intimacy.

Yet, Neal did nothing. He was all ears, but nothing else except excuses. He talked about how, "He was never taught what a marriage was growing up," as if his wife wasn't allowing him the opportunity to learn despite the fact he should have learned before getting married. He ignored every bit of guidance on showing compassionate empathy because it felt too "one-sided," though he never had a problem being one-sided when the one side was his.

He betrayed her, and she extended grace, while he thanked her with temper tantrums because the process called for him to improve as a man. While I hoped for the best, I wasn't surprised at the inevitable, but Carol was crushed. That was, until I explained to her that the intramarital healing process had actually worked.

The primary goal of healing together without hurting each other is to end up healed. It provides a way to do it together, but that's not the priority. Healing is.

While I 100% am in favor of two people keeping their marriage and removing the actions and mindsets that hurt their marriage, I also understand that if a person is clinging to their mindset that hurt you, then losing them isn't a loss.

Safely guiding a man into your healing process will automatically weed him out if he's committed to being unsafe. He will repeat the same infraction, take it to new heights, or just abort mission altogether.

This is why self-love isn't an alternative to healing within a relationship, but the catalyst to doing it the right way. It's not something you do when there's no one there to love you, but rather raises the quality of the love that you'll allow in. This means loving yourself enough to both guide a qualified person into your journey while letting the unqualified go their separate way.

Neal fell into the latter category.

It wasn't because he was a "bad" guy. Maybe he was, but that's a bit subjective and not the fundamental reason why someone isn't qualified.

Neal wasn't qualified because his comfort with the process became more important than the end goal of the process. He wanted to choose their counselor by his standards, or he wasn't going to counseling. He wanted to have sex immediately and learn the proper way to meet her sexual needs later, when he felt like it. He wanted to set the boundaries that worked for him and negotiate the others that he didn't care for.

He also wasn't qualified because Carol simply wasn't the one he truly loved. He may have married her out of convenience because he thought it's what he wanted. Nonetheless, intramarital healing only results in a healthy marriage when the offender is truly repentant, and both people see their relationship as worth the effort to restore. Emphasis on *both people*. As I've stressed repeatedly throughout this book, it takes two.

That's why I don't measure relationship success or competence by any relationship label, not even my own. You can be the most supportive, beautiful, sexiest, comforting, interesting, intelligent, hard-working, God-fearing person in the world. If you're the only one showing up to work on your marriage, it will fail. Notice, I didn't say you'll end up divorced, because many failed marriages are still celebrating anniversaries today where one spouse has completely checked out while the other is either fighting alone, or content with a loveless relationship. However, a healthy marriage requires two people who show up daily to invest in, care for, and build each other up. The same goes for the intramarital healing process if both spouses truly want their marriage to last.

Understandably, Carol had yet to see things that way, and instead had approached the depression stage of her grief over her perceived loss. The truth was she had gained so much more of what she was actually looking for.

I once heard a quote that said, "I asked God to protect me from my enemies, and then I started losing friends." I've seen the same concept apply to relationships. As people begin deepening their prayer life, asking God for a turnaround, and then co-laboring with Him to combine their faith with work, the manifestation tends to look different than what they expected, and includes much more discomfort than they were hoping for as well.

However, answered prayers are often painful in the beginning.

If you're praying for protection, you may not be able to choose whom you must be protected from. If you pray for healing, you may not be able to choose what obstruction to your healing must be removed first. If you're praying for freedom from the torment of being hurt, you may not get to choose the chains that must be broken to set you free.

In that case, those chains were her connection to Neal. Not because she wasn't good enough but because Neal fell for the 20/80 illusion.

Tyler Perry is often accredited for the original 80/20 theory, although its origins are unknown. It was made popular in today's conversation on relationships after a scene in his movie *Why Did I Get Married?* included a life lesson on how getting 80% of what you need from a marriage constitutes a great marriage because no one can provide the full 100%. However, some of us go after someone else's 20% and end up losing our 80% we had to begin with. I believe this is true, and would even take it a step further to explain why those who end up chasing the 20% are fooled into thinking it is the 80% they need.

This would be the 20/80 illusion, a perspective on someone that's based on how well they supplement current needs being met while giving the illusion that it's a worthy replacement.

It's like coffee being a great way to get some extra energy, but food and water is the true source of our body's energy. Food and water give us 80% of what we need, but if someone doesn't know any better, they'll look at the energy coffee gives and think, "This is what I *really* need. Not food." The 20/80 illusion makes us forget that if it wasn't for food and water, we'd be dead. Even though coffee gives a little boost, it's not the real engine. With proper diet, water, exercise, and rest, we don't even need coffee to get through our day, nor do we have to worry about the "crash" from consuming coffee.

In a relationship, "coffee" is forbidden, so it shouldn't even be an option, but for those who haven't set that standard, they set themselves up for the "crash." A person outside the relationship may seem like a better option, but the vantage point is deceptively shallow since the one who's in the relationship is operating with many needs currently met. They may take those met needs for granted and therefore forget that they're being met, but they are.

So, in Carol and Neal's marriage, Carol took care of their child. Neal didn't have to worry about their daughter being put in dangerous situations, neglected, or mistreated in any way. Neal also had a cooked meal at least five days a week, two to three times a day. This freed his time to work and relax as needed while getting fed like royalty. Neal never had to worry about being embarrassed when out in public with family because Carol carried herself with such class. She was faithful, respectful, and ordinarily submissive to Neal's leadership in the home. He also could trust Carol with their finances because she was frugal and intentional about her spending.

However, Neal hated that Carol wouldn't send him sexy photos when he was at work, nor did she love when Neal would send her photos of his progress in the gym. Sometimes she'd outright ignore them as well as any photos he posted online. He begged her to dress a little sexier at night, but Carol simply didn't feel comfortable walking around in the lingerie and high heels that he desired so deeply. It was much easier chasing after their toddler in her bonnet and old worn-out pajamas she'd had since college.

This may seem petty, but this was a legitimate gripe for Neal who was very visual and needed that stimulation to feel satisfied and desired in the relationship. However, his unwillingness to resolve the issue the right way made him a prime candidate to fall for the 20/80 illusion. Then one day while sifting through the "likes" on a recent post of his, he stuck his foot squarely between the teeth of that trap as he discovered Laura.

She'd "liked" the last several months' worth of photos on Neal's page and flaunted several sexy lingerie photos. She even posted captions admonishing women who didn't do any and everything to satisfy their husbands in the bedroom. You know, those "lazy" women who dare thought it was okay to gain five pounds and go a day without makeup. She preached about how second nature it was for her to continue staying in tip-top shape, and how she felt naked without a full face of makeup and freshly done hair at all times. Bonnets were forbidden in her nightly attire and high-heeled shoes were a must for so much as a trip to the refrigerator.

This was music to Neal's sore eyes, and when he sent her a message to show appreciation for her posts, their emotional affair was born.

Laura spoke life into Neal. She affirmed his sexual needs and caressed his ego like it was a Siberian kitten. She told him his photos were impeccable and begged him for more. She sent him photos as a part of her pep talk to start his day since he'd begun telling Laura about his marital woes with Carol.

Neal had everything he thought he needed with Laura, but not everything he needed *from* Laura. Big difference.

Yet it would seem he got more and more from her the more his investment in her resulted in distance from Carol. So, when Carol discovered his emotional affair and demanded he end it if he didn't want to lose his family, he verbally committed to the process except there was an issue that wasn't verbalized. He was not only emotionally attached to his affair partner, but also disillusioned into believing the best thing to ever happen to him, Carol, was the problem.

She was the one complaining, while Laura showered him with praises. She was the one asking him to change while Laura "loved" him just as he was. She was the one who ignored his posts online while Laura would write compliments that rivaled hot and sexy scenes from a romance novel about how his posts made her feel.

From Neal's perspective, Carol was getting in the way of all those moments of bliss he had with Laura becoming his full-time reality when the truth was, Carol's continued presence in his life shielded him from all the ways Laura was nowhere close to a replacement for her.

Neal subconsciously gave Laura credit for much of the comforts Carol was providing, and like a leap towards a pretty butterfly off the edge of a cliff, Neal went for the illusion that Laura was the one.

Well, about forty days after Carol found his note of resignation from the marriage, she received a flood of emails from Neal apologizing for leaving. He professed that he was officially done with his rendezvous with Laura and wanted to come back home. He was ready to be all that Carol needed and more. He expressed how deeply sorry he was for all he'd put Carol through and promised to do whatever it took to make it work.

I sat on the phone with Carol, listening in pure amusement as she explained how it all came full circle.

"But Neal didn't know that I was still logged into his iCloud from the first time I found out he was dealing with her," she continued. "Oh, the occasional flirtation and sexting dried up real quick when he called one night and kept getting ignored. He even got jealous that she would copy and paste the same compliments she sent him to other guys. I suppose since he wasn't at home pretending I was the problem, he had more time on his hands to investigate what was really going on with her. He must've thought he was special. "

I took a sip of my tea, no longer taking notes to guide her through to an understanding on her hurtful situation, but rather genuinely glued to hear the rest of how this unfolded.

She went on, "And then, he never got a new credit card, so I could see his statements showing that he'd flown out to see her. He sent a few dollars to her to come out here, but she made excuse after excuse, so he just flew out to the UK and saw her. Well guess what, she wasn't all she was cracked up to be. In fact, she was actually a "he."

I spit out my tea and we both laughed hysterically.

Neal was regretful for his decision for all the wrong reasons, and being that it wasn't a genuine repentant heart but rather humiliation and disappointment that led to him trying once more with Carol, she rejected his effort to start over. But it further confirmed the power of the 20/80 illusion. He was so unaware of how many of his basic needs Carol met while hyper focusing on her deficiencies, he ignored the boxes he didn't check off for Laura.

While this is a one-of-a-kind story, it's consistent with the statistics of those who leave a marriage for their affair partner. Only 3-5% of those relationships last long enough to become marriages, and those marriages fail 80% of the time in the first five years. That means there's about a 99% chance that when a person leaves their spouse for an affair partner, they will end up in Neal's shoes.

There are many additional reasons for that, but the moral of the story is, not everyone is cut out for this intramarital healing process, and if they aren't, you must be willing to cut them out. Sometimes the ending is as hilarious as Carol and Neal's, but other times it may not be.

There are some instances where the person walking away leaves, and it still feels like they took the best of you with them. It seems like you were never good enough to love anyway, and they're now going to move on to bigger and better things without you. Sometimes it hurts for so long you wonder if it's worth it to even get to the other side of healing, if there is a such thing.

Before I officially began writing this book, I interviewed fifty women who'd experienced this, and were now in relationships that were a complete 180-degree difference from the one they healed from. Some of these women were with new men and others with the same one who'd previously hurt them, but the 100% consensus was that it was all worth it, and then some.

I'm a firm believer that women shouldn't go through hell to get to heaven with any man, but there are some times where the "hell" part of it isn't a choice. Whether someone makes a mistake or someone is a mistake, we can find ourselves going through a painful experience we never saw coming, and to make it to our "heaven," requires a series of choices. Sometimes those choices include the choice to let someone go if they're not willing to make the right choices.

But then there are those who do make the right choices because losing you is not an option; not only losing you but allowing themselves to be any part of the reason you lose yourself trying to love them. There are men who do unfortunately start far behind the 8-ball when it comes to readiness for a healthy marriage, but given the opportunity, won't waste it in making you thank God you gave it one more chance.

There are men who see you, flaws, scars, and all, and want every bit of you and will fight hell and heaven to keep you in their lives and your heart renewed back to full strength. These men are aware of their own flaws but don't lean on them to create excuses, but rather wage all-out war against those flaws that have contributed to your pain.

Make no mistake; there are men who are stuck in their ways and best to let go. But there are also men who move mountains to save the marriage and will internally change anything that threatens the security of it going forward. *Healing Together Without Hurting Each Other* will either reveal that man in your life or make room for the one who's ready to be equipped for this fight you're in to return to and further become your best self.

However, your worthiness to be loved isn't contingent on either outcome. You were worthy before you met any man, before you were first heartbroken, and you're still worthy now.

It may not currently feel like it as the tears continue to come unexpectedly. You may have thoughts being triggered or struggle to remember what life was even like before you were hurt, but I promise you, there is life on the other side of these temporary experiences.

Just like the harvest that follows the season of back-breaking work to plant and fertilize seed, you may have had every bit of comfort in your life uprooted, but God's replanting you for an amazing harvest. The long days and nights, rain, and fertilizer may seem like more than you can handle, but you've always been stronger than you knew you were, and the same applies now. You're stronger than you currently think, and when you're tasting the sweet and satisfying fruit from this painfully long season of planting, you will look back and know that it was worth it. You are worth it.

Remember that, and let it encourage you, and find peace in that Romans 8:28 teaches us all things work together for the good of those that love the Lord. "The good" is your portion. Peace, safety, and a love that overflows from and back to you is your portion. A spouse who truly loves you and is willing to do whatever it takes to love you properly is your portion. Winning this fight for your healing is your portion.

I'm agreeing with you in faith that it is already yours. Claim it and receive it in Jesus' name.

Amen!

Epilogue:

Healing From a Covert Narcissist

After spending the last ten years dedicating my life to helping people avoid and overcome debilitating circumstances in their love lives, I realized something; things aren't always cookie cutter.

I realize that and am wise enough to know that I can't cover every issue under the sun with a one-size-fits-all approach. There are mental illnesses and childhood traumas far beyond my current capacity to deal with, and for any reason, if you feel like you still need more help than what I have provided with this book, please seek that help from a mental health professional. I share my observations from personal experience, independent research, and conclusions based on the results achieved from helping thousands of others. I've seen the proof its effectiveness to change lives and I stand firmly on it, but I also know there are some situations that require a clinical approach by a licensed professional, and I implore you to see one if you still need help, have thoughts of suicide, or believe you suffer from depression. I do not take any of those things lightly, and neither should you.

I also realize that most of the advice available does not account for those who are narcissists or show signs of suffering from Narcissistic Personality Disorder.

This is another area that isn't "cookie-cutter" as the common perception of a narcissist is one who is loud and arrogant, but the most dangerous kind of narcissist is much more passive aggressive and covert.

This person flies under the radar, but can do the same, if not more damage on a person's psyche than the traditional conception of a narcissist, because you never see them coming. They make you question your sanity, value, and your ability to function without them, giving them the power to completely ruin you little by little, over time.

I don't say this to "spook" you but if you've ever dealt with a person like this, then you know the horrors of trying to escape their mental grip. You also know that during a process of healing, they will take the very tools you're using to try and rebuild your life to dig your emotional grave.

Amidst the pain common to any healing process, it's difficult to separate the one who hurt you from someone who is out to hurt you, like a covert narcissist. So, here a few signs that may help you know if your spouse could be one:

1. **Manipulation:** While most of the signs will fall under this category, the general characterization of manipulation is any deceptive, underhanded, or indirect tactic that benefits the potential narcissist at the victim's expense. For example, instead of telling you something is bothering him, he treats you coldly for weeks leaving you to essentially beg him to let you know what's wrong. That's a form of manipulation to keep power over your imagination and also keep you at the mercy of his willingness to give you clarity.

2. **Gas lighting**: Trying to remove any certainty or confidence you have in your ability to identify with

reality or recall memories by means of telling you lies or questioning you until you doubt what you already know. An example of this is completely dismissing your feelings about his tardiness to a family event and instead telling you that you're overreacting or completely making things up despite you knowing for a fact that he was late. Over time, this erodes your confidence in what you absolutely, without a shadow of a doubt, would normally know.

3. **Harming your reputation:** Going to family and friends, social media, or any social circle and positioning you in a bad light whether by complete falsehood, a distortion of real experiences behind the guise of "his truth," or overemphasis on a legitimately negative quality devoid of context. For example, he calls you "crazy" because you went through his phone, but he leaves out the part about his phone blowing up with phone calls at night that he refused to answer in front of you. Therefore, your distrust was negative, but it was also warranted. Yet, without context, it wrongfully makes you out to be the villain.

4. **Those with differences are seen as inferior:** If there is a default disdain towards those with different strengths and weaknesses, struggles, pasts, levels of education, money, career titles, etc., your spouse may be a covert narcissist. To some extent, we all fear what we don't understand and prefer to stay in familiar surroundings or around those who share similar interests, but unwarranted dislike for a person without knowing them is a sign that a person holds a deep-seeded belief of superiority.

5. **High sense of entitlement:** Other people, you included, must work hard to earn the thing the covert

narcissist believes they should be freely given. By default of their own idea of themselves, they "deserve" empathy, consideration, or preferential treatment from others and resent anyone who challenges that notion.

6. **Passive aggressive punishment:** While overt narcissists will blatantly retaliate as a form of punishment, covert narcissist do so underhandedly and often "play dumb" about doing it. Instead of assertively communicating boundaries or whatever consequences should come as a response to something you've done, there will be an undeniable negative response to something you've done or said, but when you bring it up, they will pretend nothing is wrong. This is a form of gas lighting and manipulative control over your imagination to keep you guessing.

7. **Their failures always relate to you:** Whatever disappointment they have somehow seems to be related to a sacrifice that was made for you or something that wouldn't have happened if it wasn't for you. If they're not blaming you, they're comparing their failures to your unfair advantages in life, but somehow, you get tied in as either the excuse for their shortcomings, or the one they're seemingly competing with. Most people may relate their failures to their partner in a way that thanks their partner for their support in that time. A covert narcissist will say something like, "I could've made it to the NBA but you always had a problem with me going to practice, so here I am," or, "If only I had a rich daddy like you to put me through college."

8. **Arguments go in circles:** This is a lesser-known tactic of a covert narcissist that's used to frustrate or

confuse the victim so that any effort to validate feelings is met with failure. Especially in cases where the covert narcissist is being held accountable, you'll notice there are multiple deflections, "shutting down" behavior, or other things that pull the attention away from the conversation to avoid any real resolution. If you notice that in every conversation, attention must shift to why your partner isn't listening, or their reasoning for their hurtful actions changes every time you reveal its problematic nature, or even a sarcastic "okay, you win," to end the conversation without validating themselves as actually being wrong, but rather that they're the ones tired of arguing, these are all tactics of a covert narcissist to spin you in circles with a conversation. Even though the latter scenario ends a conversation, it's meant to prevent true resolution and closure on the topic which keeps your mind spinning on the topic and therefore leaves you in even worse of a position than what you were before the conversation.

The list of signs of a covert narcissist goes on and on, and if you even suspect you could be dealing with one, it's important that you learn them all. We spend years of our lives learning about the Pythagorean theorem and molecular structures of plants. The least we can do is learn the signs, preventative measures, and healing strategies of dealing with the very real threat of narcissists.

This book is not to be used when dealing with one of these, but if you want to know how to, and most importantly, how to break free from a covert narcissist once and for all, I recommend you take my Narcissistic Detox Master Class.

This is a class I've taught in the past for $997 but will make available for free for the first 10,000 people who purchase this book in honor of this being the tenth book in my collection after ten years in my career.

To get free access to this master class, go to **narcdetox.com**.

This class covers the ways to identify a covert narcissist, combat their malicious efforts to break you, and fully recover from the time you spent trying to love them.

As you may know, when leaving a covert narcissist, you aren't just leaving them, but rather leaving the way they hurt you, taught you to see the world, and the way they taught you to see yourself.

This is a completely different ball game than dealing with someone who's simply made some mistakes, and if you truly loved this person, you need more than even what this book can provide. I strongly encourage you to take advantage of this free offer while it lasts.

Again, the free master class is at **narcdetox.com**. The link will not work once it reaches 10,000 registrations, so hurry.

You got this, and you are not alone. The best is yet to come.

With Love,
Derrick

POPULAR BOOKS BY DERRICK JAXN

I STILL WANT IT.
(POETRY BOOK)

You can purchase by visiting <ins>www.derrickjaxn.com</ins>
Also available on Amazon, iBooks, and Nook.

POPULAR BOOKS BY DERRICK JAXN

Single Mothers are for Grown Men, ONLY!

You can purchase by visiting www.derrickjaxn.com
Also available on Amazon, iBooks, and Nook.

Card Games for Better Intimacy With Your Spouse

Lust Languages Card Game

Available at www.msmcardgame.com